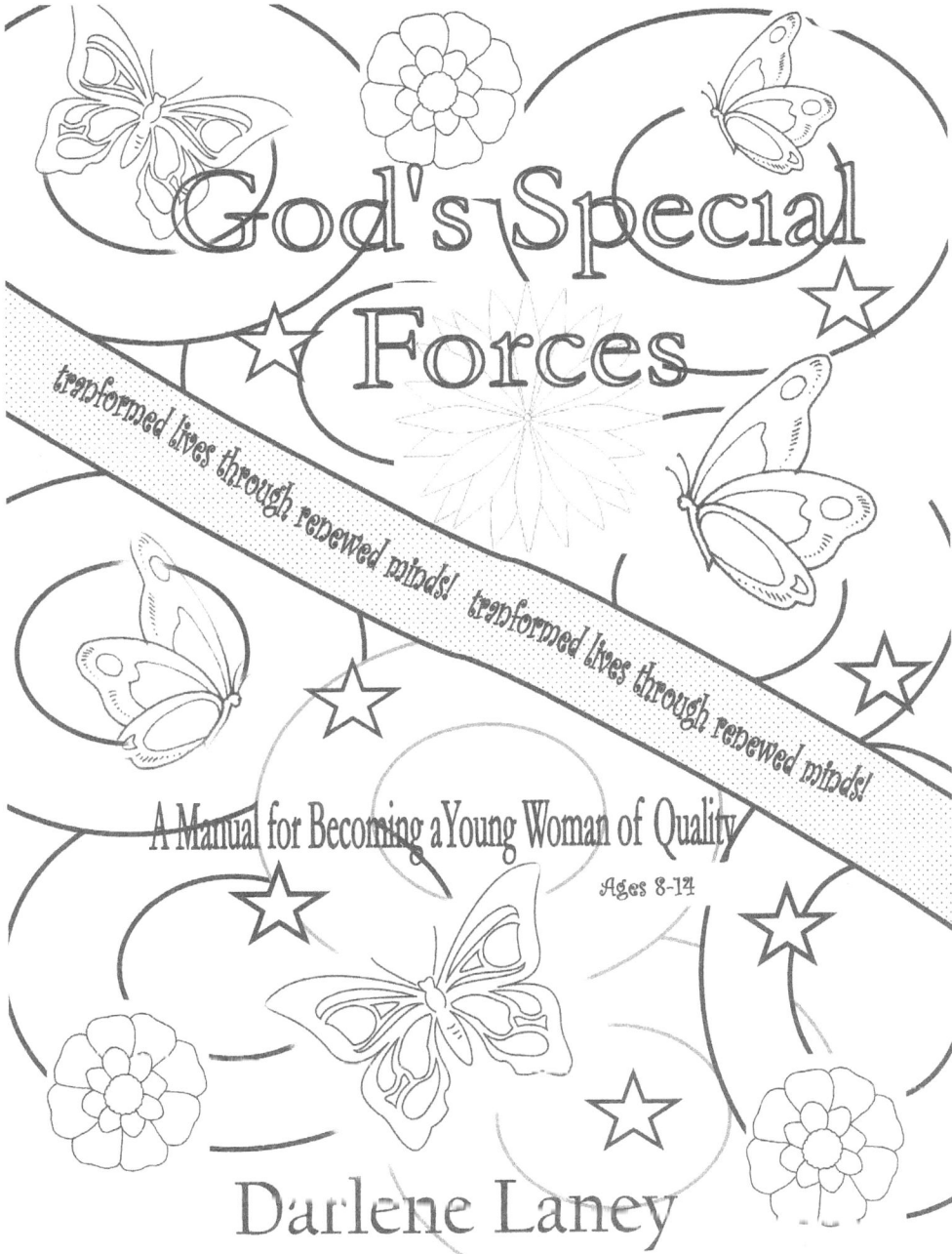

God's Special Forces

tranformed lives through renewed minds! tranformed lives through renewed minds!

A Manual for Becoming a Young Woman of Quality

Ages 8-14

Darlene Laney

Halo ●●●●
Publishing International

God's Special Forces (GSF) Program by Darlene Laney, M.A.
Copyright © 2013 Darlene Laney
Illustrator: Darlene Laney
For more information please contact,
Author at:
E-mail: godspecialforces@inbox.com
Website: www.darlenelaney.com
To learn more about the GSF Program contact:
Website: www.godspecialforces.com
All rights reserved.

Paperback ISBN: 978-1-61244-126-9
Library of Congress Control Number: 2012923801

Printed in the United States of America

Halo ●●●●
Publishing International

Published by Halo Publishing International
AP# 726
P.O Box 60326
Houston, Texas 77205
Toll Free 1-877-705-9647
Website: www.halopublishing.com
E-mail: contact@halopublishing.com

Forward

I believe the best endorsements and recommendations are from those that have first-hand experience of the product. Below, a few of the mother's of participants in the GSF Program have written their personal statements and endorsements for the program. I am forever grateful that I had an opportunity to sow into their daughter's lives.

Even though it has been years ago and I don't remember the name of the program, I will never forget the results of the program Evangelist Darlene Laney did for the young ladies at our church. The change was dramatic. They were changed. I even now can recall the difference it made in them. It seemed they grew up overnight; their behavior changed, they were more respectful and it seemed they had more confidence in themselves. They had smiles on their faces and it seemed that they had a love for each other that had never been seen, they wanted to be helpers one to another and it seemed that they enjoyed being at church and most important of all they wanted to be like Evangelist Darlene, an educated and loving and caring woman of God. She lives the life she teaches…she stands on the Word of God and is empowered by the Holy Spirit. I highly commend Evangelist Darlene Laney for developing the GSF Program and for her faithfulness and contributions to young girls from all walks of life.

Beverly McAlister – 1st Lady
Powerhouse Church of God in Christ
(October 2012)

God's Special Forces

God's Special Forces is a very special and unique program designed to teach young ladies how to be ladies. It's more than just a charm school. God's Special Forces works on the girl's self-esteem and uses the Word of God to speak the truth about who she really is. The work is done within the heart of the young lady and then is transferred to the actions of the young lady. We are God's creation dearly loved, the Bride of Christ. God's Special Forces teaches young ladies how to present themselves to the world. Evangelist Laney teaches with such elegance and style it becomes transformable into the lives of these young women. God's Special Forces is a must have class for all young ladies.

Debra Walker
Central Valley Community Bank
SBA Credit Analyst

Arise ye daughters of Zion!

The practical/biblical instruction received from this manual will equip young ladies with the skills to live out the call upon their lives to be Mighty Women of God.

Minister Tarole Pettigrew
West Side Church of God

Dedication

There are many people that come into our lives. Some come to bring inspiration, some bring adversity. There are others that bring love and challenges. Then there are those that are there for you, no matter what. They don't allow you to settle and just get by or half do and consider it done. No, there are some that come into our lives to support us, push us, encourage us and at times make us angry. But, whatever their purpose, I believe they are there to make us better.

I call them God's sandpaper. I thank God that I've been blessed to have such women in my life. These women have not allowed me to just get by or be satisfied with mediocrity; rather they have challenged me and demanded the best that I had to give. Because of them, I was able to take what they imparted into me and turn it into a self-esteem enhancing program for girls. Girls that were like me, shy, inept, and lacking in social grace. To each of them, I give recognition and my heartfelt thanks.

To Mrs. Flo Atwater, a retired professional model that taught me how to stand with my head high and my back straight; to walk with dignity and sit like a lady.

To Ms. Christine Jennings for all the time she spent teaching Purity Class preparing us for a time when we would need to know how to shake hands and properly introduce others. Thank you for teaching us proper etiquette and table manners. And, thank you especially for demonstrating to us true elegance and poise.

And, lastly to my mother, Mrs. Corrine Madden-White for all the encouragement, support and opportunities she gave me. Without her, this book would not have come to fruition; there would be no GSF and no *Young Women of Quality.* I want others to know that it was my mom that walked beside me through neighborhoods passing out flyers announcing GSF is coming during the hot Fresno summer. It was my mom that was there for my first GSF meeting with only three girls in attendance. When I was discouraged, she told me to just keep on going. It was my mom that traveled with me throughout the San Joaquin Valley as I spread the word that *He Made a Woman.* It was my mom that believed in me when I did not believe in myself. Thank you Mom, so very much! I love you and I miss you greatly.

Introduction

Welcome to *God's Special Forces* (GSF) a dynamic program, that will enhance your self-esteem, teach you proper etiquette and develop your social skills. The GSF Program is an 11-lesson, biblically-based, program for girls between the ages of 8-14 years that will challenge and encourage you to "step out of the status quo, take off the old and put on the new!" Throughout the program, GSF will introduce you to new and exciting information and provide practice exercises that will help you acquire poise and grace.

As a facilitator of the GSF workshop: "Mirror, Mirror, on the Wall," and the 11 lesson program, I can say with confidence that you will see *change* after the first session! Your parents, friends and others will notice the change in only two sessions. How do I know? Many past participants of this program have told me that the information they received changed the way they thought and acted because it was important and key to their transformation.

Throughout this program, GSF will present you with information that will energize your thinking and *change* the way you see yourself. Additionally, you will be given the opportunity to put into practice the new ideas you will be learning. The practice sessions will **empower** (make powerful), **nurture** (develop) and **affirm** (support) you. By the end of the program you will *walk with your head high and your back straight*, knowing that you *are somebody, because God don't make no junk*! Each lesson will give you information and provide you with the experiences that will help you become the capable and confident young woman God intended you to be. What you do with the information is up to you.

So whether you are going through the workbook on your own, or are a part of a GSF group, welcome to an exciting journey of empowerment and transformation!

Table of Contents

LESSON ONE – A NEW LOOK WITHIN AND WITHOUT

"Far better it is to dare mighty things, to win glorious triumphs, even though checkered by failure, than to take rank with those poor spirits who neither enjoy nor suffer much because they live in the gray twilight that knows neither victory nor defeat."

Theodore Roosevelt

Beauty is not just about what's on the outside. True beauty begins on the inside and radiates out. The GSF Program is designed to provide you with information and experiences that will assist you in being truly beautiful.

God's Special Forces' (GSF's) slogan is *"transformed lives through renewed minds."* By following the instructions as outlined in this course and participating in the activities provided, you will find that you will be ***transformed*** which simply means to be changed into the unique and beautiful creation God intended you to be! However, before we get started, let me give you a preview of what you can expect and what GSF expects from you.

YOU CAN EXPECT:

1. To have a *new look* - You will receive instruction in basic beauty techniques that will help to give you a *new look*—a look that is uniquely you not just outwardly but inwardly as well. Your inward look will be built on sound Biblical principles, and your outward look will consist of basic beauty techniques, good nutrition and basic social skills. You will discover and learn how to use the most powerful beauty technique known to womankind to ensure that you not only look good but feel good as well.

2. To be uniquely *you*- Have you ever wanted to look like or be like your favorite movie star or video star? Have you ever wished you had been born with blue eyes instead of brown, or that you were tall and slim instead of petite and plump? If you are like most girls, you will answer *yes* to these questions. Unfortunately, the majority of girls your age are not satisfied with the way they look and spend a lot of time and effort trying to imitate others.

Jeremiah 1:5 says in part, "Before I formed you in the womb, I knew thee." God says that he knew you while you were growing in your mother's womb. He knew what color your eyes would be; He knew how tall you would be; He even knew you would be a girl and not a boy. He knew all of this before your conception (formed in the womb).

You are no accident and it is not by random selection that you look the way you look. You are an individual miracle of God; fearfully and wonderfully made in His image and likeness. You are to be celebrated because out of all the millions of people on this earth, there is no other like you.

If you are not satisfied with who you are, GSF will help you to discover why you are not satisfied with who you are and will then give you some vital(very important) information that will help you learn to celebrate you for the unique creature you are. This information will help you realize that what you take in affects how you feel about yourself and how you feel effects how you view yourself. The way you view yourself in turn effects what you do. You will also learn that true beauty begins on the inside and radiates to the outside. True beauty allows you to be uniquely you.

3. To have more confidence - The tips and suggestions given to you regarding the styles best suited for your figure type, what hairstyle compliments your unique face shape, how to stand, walk and sit, combined with up-to-date basic tips on proper etiquette will give you the tools to successfully navigate whatever social challenge you encounter not only with grace and poise but also looking your best.

As you take in the new information presented through this course and learn to master each new exercise, you will feel more capable and confident. In other words, you will have more confidence thus boosting your self-esteem.

WHAT GSF EXPECTS FROM YOU:

1. Give your best!

As you enter the GSF training program, you are entering a place of change and a place to practice new ways of being and doing. During the time you spend in the program, GSF will help you on the road to becoming all God created you to be. The program starts with you, just as you are today. You will be asked to do some very challenging things and set goals. No matter how difficult the task, assignment, or exercises, know that each is designed to bring you closer to becoming a Young Woman of Quality.

GSF expects you to set goals for yourself. At first, this might seem like a very difficult task. However, after a short period of time, you will find yourself looking forward to this exercise. Reaching your goals will depend largely on how much time and effort you are willing to put into their accomplishment. Fear not; you are not alone. Your GSF team will be there to help you every step of the way.

If you're going through the program book on your own, you will be able to accomplish your goals if you faithfully read each lesson and then complete and practice all the exercises, as presented. One suggestion: allow at least one week for each lesson. And, if you have questions or concerns, email me at: godspecialforces@inbox.com. Or, if you have a question and want to have it discussed on the GSF blog—*Something to Talk About* just go to www.godspecialforces.com.

You will find that the GSF Program is divided into 11 lessons or modules. Each module covers a particular aspect of beauty and charm, ranging from *The Beginning* and concluding with *Putting It All Together*. Ideally, the lessons are to be presented on a weekly basis utilizing role-play, videos, lectures and guest speakers to provide instruction in helping you become all that you were created to be. You can find out more by contacting me. However, you can complete the program on your own by following the instructions and faithfully practicing the exercises.

In order to get the maximum benefits from this program, you must be committed. In other words, if you are part of a GSF group, you have to commit to being present and on time, or if you're going through the booklet on your own, you will need to set aside at least an hour each week to do the program.

For those of you attending a GSF program at the first meeting, you will be asked, "Are you committed to reaching your goals and becoming all that you were purposed to be?" If you are in agreement, you will be asked to sign an *I'M COMMITTED* card or sign the *I'M COMMITTED* pledge at the end of this chapter.

For those of you going through the booklet on your own, the *I'm Committed* card is included in the booklet. If you want to become a member of the GSF Program, please complete the card and send it to me at: *God's Special Forces*, P.O. Box 3654, Pinedale, California 93650-3654

2. Be Yourself!

Once you have committed to GSF, we'll ask you to go one step further—always be yourself. GSF is not designed to assist you in becoming a carbon copy of your favorite star or to teach you to walk like a fashion model. Rather, GSF values the uniqueness of each individual and will work with you in discovering and accentuating your particular uniqueness. Just as God did not make any two snowflakes alike, He did not make any two people alike. Therefore, no matter how tempting it is to be like someone else, you must commit to strive to be uniquely you.

3. Free Yourself!

I encourage you to start now to give yourself permission to try out and practice the exercises suggested in this manual. Now is the time to examine your old way of thinking and challenge yourself to take in new information. You will be introduced to some not so familiar ideas, and in some cases, re-introduced to some familiar ideas! GSF encourages you to start now to give yourself permission to experiment and enjoy what we believe to be an uplifting and liberating experience.

Are you ready? Then let's get started, at the beginning!

On Your Mark!
Get Ready!
Get Set!
GOOOOOOOO!

LESSON TWO – THE BEGINNING

"When you make a mistake, don't look back at it long. Take the reason of the thing into your mind and then look forward. Mistakes are lessons of wisdom. The past cannot be changed. The future is yet in your power..."
Hugh White

In the Beginning

In order to go forth, it is necessary to look to the past to determine the beginning. Some of you might be thinking that *the beginning* referred to here was when you were being fearfully and wonderfully made in your mother's womb.

"Before I formed thee in the belly I knew thee..."Jeremiah 1:5

No, this beginning was long before you were conceived. As a matter of fact it was long before your mother was conceived; your mother's mother was conceived and even before your grandmother's mother was conceived.

The beginning I'm referring to in this chapter was a long, long time ago. It began with creation – the very beginning of time. Have you heard of the Creation Story—Adam and Eve. Well that is where it all began. If you have not already done, so take time to *read Genesis, Chapters 1 and 2* before beginning this lesson. It will give you the background information you need to understand this lesson. As you read the Creation account, pay attention to the words used in describing how the earth, the creatures of the earth and man and woman were brought into existence.

Creation, as recorded in Genesis, began with God **speaking** (Gen.1:3). Then it continued when He brought man into Creation by **forming** (Gen. 2:7) him and breathing into him the breath of life; and ended with God **making** (Gen. 2:22) a woman. These words are significant and can only be understood by searching out their meaning.

In creating the earth and the inhabitants of the earth, as we know them today, God used three distinctly different methods. I don't know about you but I don't know a lot about the language the Bible was written in, so I consult a dictionary…the Strong's Concordance. I hope you will practice this also. If you come across a word in the Bible or any other book, stop and look the word up in a concordance or a dictionary. I know, it takes time but it is definitely time well spent. Take a look at what I discovered just by looking up the word "made."

He Made a Woman

The word *made* **(banah)** comes from the Hebrew language and according to the Strong's Concordance means *"to skillfully shape (which implies special handling) with a specific purpose in mind."* Learning the definition in the language of its origin, you gain a broader understanding about fe-males. God made, or skillfully shaped, the female with a specific God-ordained purpose in mind. Okay, now let's go back to Genesis 2:18. Here we find another unusual word used to describe woman: *helpmeet.*

Helpmeet is a compound word which comes from the root word *azar* (awzar) and is defined in the Hebrew dictionary as to "surround and protect." *Helper,* according to Webster's New World Dictionary, implies *"to come along side and provide assistance."* The word *aide* refers to *"a person assigned to provide assistance; more particularly provide assistance to a high-ranking military official."* For example, a general in the military is assigned an aide. The duties and responsibilities of the aide are many and varied; however, his/her main responsibility is to keep the general on track by providing a buffer between him and those who would seek to distract him. In other words, no one gets to see the general until first going through the aide. The aide in essence *surrounds and protects* the general and is a vital line of defense.

Stop for a moment and think about this. Before making woman God said, *"Let us make man a helpmeet."* In other words, combining the definition supplied by Webster's, and the Biblical definition; God said, "Let us skillfully form and shape man a helper that will aide, assist, surround and protect him."

The Importance of a Rib

It is not by accident that these words are used when describing the place that God has given to woman. Nor is it by accident that God made woman from the rib of man. In creating her position as a helper that surrounds and protects, there was only one bone that could be used—the rib.

The rib cage as you know is vital in the skeletal structure. The ribs not only support the skeletal structure but also surround and protect the lungs, heart and digestive systems. Should something get through the ribs and penetrate any of these vital life-preserving organs, the organism would be mortally wounded.

Think about it.

God took a rib, the closest thing to a man's heart and that which surround and protects his very life source and He made woman!

You are special! In the beginning God created, the heavens and the earth; God formed man; and God made a woman. He skillfully formed and shaped you with a specific purpose in mind. He made you special to carry out your special role in creation.

Before you leave the creation experience, I want to make one other point. In Genesis, we find that after God created woman, man and woman came together in the Garden that God had planted (Genesis 2:25). They came together to carry out their divine given roles, Man as the tender of the garden with dominion over all and Woman as man's helpmeet, suitable and compatible in every way sharing dominion over all. And, God said, "***It is very good.***" And He rested. Ecclesiastes 3:11 in part says:

"He has made everything beautiful in its time…"

He Rested

God rested on the seventh day (Genesis 2:2). Creation was complete, perfect (very good). Adam was no longer alone. He had a helpmeet suitable in every way—bone of his bone, flesh of his flesh. Adam called her, Woman

"The man said, "This is now bone of my bones and flesh of my flesh; she shall be called woman, for she was taken out of man." (Genesis 2:23)

You Are Special

Yes, you are special. You were made special. Special care and handling went into your creation. Take a moment to think about that statement. Really think about it. Get a picture in your mind of just how beautiful, unique and special you are to God. Now that you have a picture of who you are in God's eyes, begin today to practice seeing yourself as God sees you. Look into His mirror and know that you are special in His sight. Instead of focusing on what you consider to be your flaws, celebrate them for they are what separates you and makes you unique. Start each day proclaiming, ***"I am special. I am skillfully formed and shaped by the hands of God for His specific ordained purpose."***

God's Special Forces

Because of the *specialness* that went into the making of woman, I liken women to the *Special Forces* within the armed services. *Special Forces* are assigned tasks that are not performed by any other division.

Not everyone can be a member of these elite teams. These teams are comprised of individuals who have exemplary natural skills and abilities that make them suitable for these specialized divisions. Understand something, *Special Forces* are not just sent out based upon their natural skills and abilities. They are first trained. In fact, they are put through strenuous specialized training that takes their natural skills and abilities and hones them into well-tuned, fully equipped specialized individuals. Once trained, they are fully prepared and equipped to carry out their special assignments.

Why Send a Man to do a Woman's Job?

You, young woman are:

G   **God's** (Genesis 1:1). In the beginning God. Jehovah, Yahweh, Elohim, Adonai, God.

S   **Special** (Genesis 2:22) *made* (*banah*) skillfully formed and shaped (implies special handling).

F   **Forces** (Psalms 68:11)……great was the *company* (forces) of those that published it.

You have been assigned a mission-Mission Him-possible-to carry forth His message. This mission is special to only you. The duties and responsibilities assigned are those purposed by your Maker. He made you and in your making prepared you for the mission before you. He has equipped you with all the requisite natural skills and abilities and is now providing the training you need that will hone you into a well-tuned, fully equipped Young Woman of Quality, armed and ready to serve.

No other creature on earth can carry out your mission. Just as no other creature created or formed by God could be a helpmeet to man, no created or formed creature can carry out the special duties and responsibilities assigned to you—Young Woman. Your next step is to get the information you need to learn to be who He wants you to be and fulfill your God-ordained purpose.

Whatever He has ordained for you to do, be it a homemaker training up the next generation of Christians; a doctor, lawyer, teacher or scientist, whatever your mission may be, you have resident within you all that you need to be successful.

"His divine power has given us everything we need for a godly life through our knowledge of him who called us by his own glory and goodness."
(II Peter 1:3).

Did you know you are a work of art? You are God's workmanship, his work of art created in Christ Jesus for good works which He prepared beforehand that you should walk in them. In some books masterpiece is referred to as *poetry*. So you can also say; you are poetry in motion.

"For we are God's masterpiece. He has created us anew in Christ Jesus, so we can do the good things He planned for us long ago."
Ephesians 2:10 (New Living Translation)

God has a plan and a purpose for you—good things. All you need to do to realize what is within you is to pull it out. That comes through training! Like the military Special Forces, you need to be trained. GSF can provide the instructions for that training. GSF will help you acquire many of the basic skills and give you resources you need to fulfill your purpose with poise and grace. It is up to you to put these skills to use.

Training

Have you participated in a team sport? Did you go through a training period before you played your first game? Once you were on the team did you have to continue training? You know that in training, you are going to have to exert some effort setting goals and working towards those goals. And, you will have to learn to work in a group. You and your teammates cannot be in competition with each other if you expect to be successful. You will need to learn from each other and celebrate each other's successes. Any progress you make will not come about because you wish or hope. No, your progress comes because you have determined in your mind to bring about the change and because you practice, practice, practice. As you consistently work toward your goal, change will come.

Getting Started – Basics

Let's begin by looking at ourselves and each other. Stand before a mirror and look at yourself. Really look at yourself. You might find this exercise to be a little awkward, if so take a deep breath; close your eyes and slowly open them again. Now, begin by looking closely at your face- the shape of your face, your nose, the color of your eyes, etc. Look at your hair and how it frames your face. This exercise is to start you observing *you*. Open your eyes. Stop. Close your eyes again and this time get a mental picture of yourself as you appeared in the mirror. What did you like about yourself? What did you dislike? You don't have to answer, just think about it. Okay, stop. Open your eyes. For the next part of this exercise you will need a pencil and a piece of paper. Divide the paper into two columns. At the top of the first column write "What I Like" and at the top of the second column write "What I Would Like to Change." Now write down the things you liked most about your face and the things you would like to change in the appropriate columns. Put this list away until later.

When you did this exercise did you critically analyze yourself? Or did you compare youself with someone else? Did you not like your nose because you wished that you had Sally's nose? Or, maybe you said you would like to change your eye color because you think blue eyes are prettier than brown eyes? Did you just look away from your image because you saw nothing that pleased you?

Stop. Take a deep breath. Now close your eyes again. As you do this exercise, don't just think about it, feel it! With your eyes closed think this:

> *No other person in this room, in this city, in this state, in this nation, in this whole universe is exactly like me? I am one of a kind. Unique…fearfully and wonderfully made.*

No, there is none other like you. You really are unique. You see, when God made you there was to be no other like you. You are an original, one of a kind. You are God's masterpiece…poetry in motion! It doesn't matter if people tell you, you are the spitting image of your mother, father, sister or brother, and you are still uniquely different. Just as God did not make any two snowflakes alike, He did not make any two people exactly alike; no, not even identical twins. Yes, you are unique. You are fearfully and wonderfully made. That's something to celebrate!

> *"I praise you because I am fearfully and wonderfully made; your works are wonderful, I know that full well." Psalms 139:14*

Are you beginning to get the idea that you are someone special? Well, you are very special to God. Look what He has to say about you in the following scripture:

> *"He encircled him, He cared for him, He kept him as the apple of His eye."*
> *(Deuteronomy 32:9-10 RSV)*

Did you know you are the apple of God's eye? Still not convinced that you are special? I hope this will help to convince you. Ethel Waters coined a phrase that says, "God Don't Make Junk." I wholeheartedly agree! What about you? Well, just in case you haven't gotten it yet or after you leave here and you forget, remember this: ***"I Am Somebody, cause God don't make no junk***." I know it's not proper grammar, but it makes the point!

I want you to have the GSF-God don't make no junk poster. I've included instructions for making this poster at the end of the chapter. Do take time to make the poster and once you have completed it, hang it up! This poster will be a daily reminder of who you are! Look at it when you get up in the morning, and definitely before you go to sleep at night. Look at it any time you need a reminder. Then do something else. Confess it. That's right, tell yourself you are somebody: ***"I know I'm somebody cause God don't make no junk!"*** Tell yourself again and again. Say it when you feel good. Say it when you feel bad. Say it in the morning. Say it while brushing your teeth or combing your hair. Say it in the afternoon. Say it before a test. Say it before you go to bed. Whatever you do, just say it! *I KNOW I'M SOMEBODY CAUSE GOD DON'T MAKE NO JUNK!*

Prayer:

Thank you Father for this day and the opportunity to learn and practice being the person You made me to be. Thank You for giving me all the resources, gifts and talents, I need to fulfill my purpose. Father thank You for making me a woman for I am fearfully and wonderfully made. You didn't make another one like me. No one can be me better than me.

Father thank You for the strength and courage to walk forward in your love and protection, knowing I am special to You—the apple of your eye. Thank you Father for allowing me to bring glory to you by being all that you have made me to be. Amen

Things to Do:

As you go through the week **tell yourself**:

- I am fearfully and wonderfully made
- I am unique, one of a kind
- There is none like me
- I am God's masterpiece
- I know I'm somebody Cause God don't make no junk!

Read:

Genesis Chapters 1 and 2; 1 Samuel 16:7

- ♥ **Get Creative**
  Make your own "I'm Somebody Poster."

Instructions: (To be completed on the computer)
- ♥ Start with a 8-1/2" x 11" sheet of paper
- ♥ Type the words, "I Know I'm Somebody" using a fun

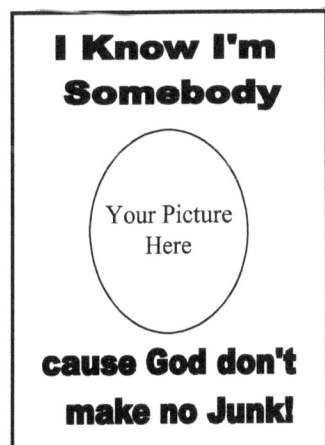

I Know I'm Somebody

Your Picture Here

cause God don't make no Junk!

font (like Curlz MT)
Remember: make the letters large. (This is a poster)

♥ Get a photo of yourself.

♥ Glue it in the center of the page.

♥ *Optional: Take your poster to your local copy center and have it enlarged.*
Remember: Be creative!

Chapter Review

Review what you've learned. Complete the questions below.

1. What were the three methods God used in creation?

   a)_____   b)_____   c)_____

2. God _____ a woman. What is the Hebrew word?_____

   What does it mean?_____

3. What did God say about creation before "He rested?" _____

   _____

4. According to Psalms 139:14, you are _____ and_____made.

5. Ethel Waters says, "you are somebody because._____

   _____

Journal (Write about what you have learned in GSF to date.)

"My heart is inditing a good matter: I speak of the things
which I have made touching the king: my tongue is the pen
of a ready writer." Psalm 45:1

Take time now to write your own devotional. Don't be discouraged if at first it seems difficult. With practice, as with anything, you will soon find that the words just flow.

Devotional

I Chronicles 16:12: Remember his marvelous works which He has done, His wonders, and the judgments of his mouth.

Affirmation: *I will remember His marvelous works which He has done, His wonders and the judgments of His mouth.*

Sometimes it's difficult to remember just how special you are to God especially when you're facing a challenging situation at school, home or wherever it might be. Today, take time to reflect on what you've learned from this first chapter.

Remember that you are beautifully *made* fearfully formed and shaped by the hand of God for good things. You are the apple of His eye and He knows everything about you. He looks at you and says: *Very good*. You are His and as a parent is proud of their child, so God is proud of you, His daughter.

Others only see the outside but God sees it all—the inside as well as the outside. He is not surprised by the things you do, even when you get angry and say the wrong thing or allow yourself to be pressured by your peers to do something that you should not do.

Take time now to ask God to forgive you for those things. Receive His forgiveness and the strength He will give you to take a stand and do the right thing the next time you're confronted with the same or a similar situation.

LESSON THREE – FACE FACTS
Mirror, Mirror, on the Wall, Am I the Fairest of Them All?

"People are like stained-glass windows. They sparkle and shine when the sun is out, but when the darkness sets in; their true beauty is revealed only if there is a light from within." *Kahil Gibram*

Beauty

Lovely, attractive, good looking, and exquisite are but a few of the words used to define beauty. Yet, according to a survey commissioned by *Dove*, 77% of girls between the ages of 10 and 14 did not use these terms in describing themselves. Rather, they identified themselves as being ugly and fat in comparison to the images they saw in magazines and media ads.

I hope you are not among this 77%. And, if you are, remember what you learned in Chapter One. You learned that you are "fearfully and wonderfully made and there is no other like you" (Psalms 139:14). You are unique, one of a kind, an original, God's masterpiece. Hopefully, you are no longer comparing yourself to the images in the magazines. If you are, here's another interesting fact that was discovered; it only takes three minutes of looking at those girls in the magazines to make you feel like an *ugly duckling*. (*my term*).

The next exercise might make you uncomfortable. But remember, that is what GSF is all about—stepping outside of your comfort zone. I want you to look at the girls around you. Take your time. Okay, now, that you've had an opportunity to look at each other, tell me, what did you look at first? Their clothes, their eyes, or maybe you said their face. If you said the first thing you notice about another person is their face then you are among the majority of those responding to this question.

The face is significant because in our society it is usually the basis we use to determine

beauty. Our ideas of beauty come from different sources, one of which is the media. Media is television, videos, magazines, movies and the like. The media would have you believe that beauty is to be determined by the images of movie stars, pop divas and supermodels seen plastered on popular magazine covers, in videos, in the movies and on television. These **icons** (*representations or images*) of beauty are presented as having those physical traits such as eye color, hair color, lips, noses, body size and the like that are deemed to be necessary to be considered beautiful. However, there is another source from which you can get an idea of what beauty is…the Bible.

The Bible has quite a different perspective on beauty. Remember Ecclesiastes 3:11:

"Yet God has made everything beautiful for its own time…" **(My emphasis)**
And, Proverbs 31:30 refers to beauty as *fleeting*.

"…beauty is fleeting; but a woman who fears the LORD is to be praised."
I Timothy 2:9 cautions you about focusing strictly on what you put on but to consider the inward person as well:

"…women are to adorn themselves in respectable apparel, with modesty and self-control, not with braided hair and gold or pearls or costly attire."
And I Peter 3:4 says:

"But let your adorning be the hidden person of the heart with the imperishable beauty of a gentle and quiet spirit, which in God's sight is very precious."
It is obvious that the Bible first considers everything beautiful and secondly puts the emphasis on the hidden person instead of focusing on the outside things thought to be beautiful by our modern culture.

But the LORD said to Samuel, "Do not consider his appearance or his height, for I have rejected him. The LORD does not look at the things people look at. People look at the outward appearance, but the LORD looks at the heart." (I Samuel 16:7)
You are encouraged to let your beauty be that of an inner quality. Proverbs 11:22 has this to say:

"As a jewel of gold in a swine's snout so is a fair woman without discretion."

Get the picture. You can be ever so pretty, ever so beautiful but if there is no substance on the inside, no values, no virtue, no manners or morals, then you are like the Bible says, a pig with a jewel in its nose. What a picture! Hopefully, you are beginning to understand that beauty is not just about what you look like…the outward appearance. Let's go further and take a look at what really makes you beautiful; those **imperishable** (*everlasting, permanent, indestructible)* qualities.

You will need to get out a mirror for this exercise. Take the time to really look at yourself. Tell me what you focused on as you looked at your **reflection** (*likeness*) in the mirror? What did you say to yourself as you gazed at your reflection? Were you pleased with the image that looked back at you? Did you smile? Whether you smiled, frowned or hastily put the mirror away says a lot about how you think and feel about yourself. And, it also has a lot to do with how you think about another person. Unfortunately, what you have been taught to think of as beauty has been strongly influenced by the media.

When looking at these images being presented to you, you are forming ideas about yourself and others. Stop; take time to look at the images presented to you in your favorite magazine. What do you see? What does what you see mean to you? Next time you're reading your favorite magazine or watching your favorite television program pay attention to the "message" you receive. In most of the media images, you get the message that being beautiful has certain benefits, like happiness, success, traveling to exotic places, being attractive to the opposite sex and just having a great time.

The message is clear; if you look like this you are pretty. If not, you are not pretty. Young women today are so in sync with today's concept of beauty that when you look at yourself or anyone else for that matter, you unconsciously compare your facial features with those that the media has **conditioned** (*trained, familiarized*) you to believe to be pretty. Anything that falls outside these traits although not said outright is deemed as unacceptable, undesirable and definitely not "pretty."

Unfortunately, this media message is wrecking havoc with many girls self-esteem and leading to some of them taking drastic actions to fit the image being shown. One such action has to do with eating or the lack thereof. Or, eating and throwing up. Another, which is on the rise, is cosmetic surgery. Did you know American women spend billions of dollars and numerous hours on making themselves *pretty*? Some women have gone so far as to inject poisonous substances into their bodies, have ribs removed, and teeth pulled, as well as putting themselves in danger of being disfigured for life just to acquire someone's idea of physical beauty. But there is another way and it is considered to be the best kept beauty secret of all time!

The Best Kept Beauty Secret

With so much hype over physical beauty, it is no wonder a commonly known beauty fact among the industry has been forgotten. Cosmetologists, make-up artists, image consultants, cosmetic surgeons and the like all know that it is not what a woman does to alter or change her appearance that makes her beautiful, rather it is…are you ready…what a woman **thinks** of herself that makes her beautiful.

Yes, it's true. It's what you think. A popular beauty magazine ran an article about cosmetic surgery. What was interesting about the article was something the surgeon being interviewed disclosed He said that although he could erase the effects of wrong thinking, excesses and the fallout of bad habits from a woman's face, his efforts would soon be reversed if the woman did not change two things. Can you guess what two things need to change? If you said her thoughts first, you are correct. The second is a little more difficult… her lifestyle. What you think has a direct effect on what you do or your lifestyle.

You might be asking yourself what cosmetic surgery has to do with you. You're just a pre-teen or even a teenager, right? And, maybe the last thing on your mind right now is surgery. However, that is not the case for a number of teen girls. Today, surgery is being performed on teenage girls in increasing numbers. I've included an excerpt from this online report from the American Society of Plastic Surgeons, 2012:

"Teenagers who want to have plastic surgery usually have different motivations and goals… They often have plastic surgery to improve physical characteristics they feel are awkward or flawed that if left uncorrected may affect them well into adulthood. Teens tend to have plastic surgery to fit in with peers, to look similar. According to American Society of Plastic Surgeons (ASPS) statistics, **nearly 219,000 cosmetic plastic surgery procedures were performed on people age 13-19 in 2010."** *(Emphasis mine)*

That's a lot of procedures and, as this report indicates, the surgeries are performed because according to the teen-ager, it will make her feel better about herself and fit in with her peers. Because she feels better, she will have a better attitude about herself. A better attitude will lead to her doing better and doing better will lead to more success. In other words, as *she thinks, so is she*.

Don't misunderstand, there are some instances where cosmetic surgery is essential; however, my point is having surgery to fit in with peers or look similar to your peers. Too bad it requires surgery for some teenage girls to be able to do this. Wouldn't it be great to just feel better about yourself without having to undergo an expensive and many times dangerous surgical procedure? It seems it would help to learn that all the surgery or cosmetics in the world are of no benefit if you don't take proper care of the one organ that is fundamental for true beauty…the mind. Are you surprised? What does your mind have to do with beauty?

It has been said that you can read a person's life story by looking at their face. When you make facial expressions, you are essentially transmitting a lot of information that can be received, read, and interpreted by others. By various expressions, you can produce thousands of different messages. These messages give others an indication of your overall emotional state, your feelings about where you are and what you are doing, your mental well-being, your personality and mood, your physical health, as well as whether you are a good person or not.

Another way of putting it is that **your face** is a *recorder of your internal emotional state or your thoughts*. Whatever you consistently think about will show on your face. A very wise man by the name of Solomon put it this way, *"As a man thinketh in his heart, so is he."* (Proverbs 23:7)

Try it for yourself. Look in a mirror and think about someone or something that makes you really angry, sad or depressed. Notice how this alters your appearance. Notice the lines that appear on your face. Now, think about someone or something that makes you feel really good! What do you see? Does your face change with each thought? Did you know that over time these emotions will make themselves seen on your face…permanently?

What's on Your Mind?

What do you think about? Are your thoughts devaluing, diminishing and depressing? In other words, do the things you think make you feel *worthless, small and depressed?* If so, you're suffering from a bad case of the ***uglies.*** Let me explain the uglies. The uglies go something like this: "I'm not good enough; I'm not smart enough; I'm not popular enough; I'm not tall enough or thin enough." Or, "I don't have this or I don't have that." You name it, and you are not it and you do not have it.

You might tell yourself you think the way you do because that is what others have told you. In other words, you kept hearing, "you're not…" over and over again and gradually you were **conditioned** to believe that "you were not".

Today, you are going to make a change. Today, you will no longer allow someone's "you're not" become your "I am not." As you go through each day, you come in contact with many people and you are involved in numerous situations over which you have no control. This can cause you to experience many feelings, some good and some bad. You can't control what others think about you, but you can choose what you will think. You don't have to drown in the **uglies** (*devaluing, diminishing and depressing thoughts*) because you or someone else said something negative about you. You can take control of your thinking! How? By learning to guard your most valuable beauty asset, your mind, you do this by guarding your thoughts. To guard your thoughts start using the "Whatsoever Principles."

The Whatsoever Principles

Remember earlier I talked about receiving information that was empowering or gives you power. That is what the Whatsoever Principles do…give you power. Have you ever used the term *whatever*? Usually when you make a *whatever* statement it is to shrug off a negative statement that has been spoken to you, by you or about you. For instance, someone says they don't like you because….. You say *"Whatever."* You toss your hair, roll your eyes, or walk away, all to indicate you don't care. However, deep down inside you care. You want to be accepted. Unfortunately, saying *"Whatever"* doesn't take away the sting of unkind and hurtful words. In fact, a *"whatever"* statement diminishes you or takes away your power.

How many of you are familiar with the word **toxic** (*contaminated, tainted, polluted or impure*)? You hear a lot about toxicity these days. Unfortunately, toxicity is everywhere: in the air you breathe, the water you drink and even the food you eat can be toxic. It is no wonder then, that since we live in a toxic world, there are toxic people. And, toxic people say toxic things. These toxic people and the things they say to you will contaminate, taint and pollute your mind if allowed to take hold of your thinking.

Usually when someone says something negative (toxic) to you or about you, the tendency is to believe that it's your fault the person made the negative remark. Questions you might ask are, "What did I do?" or "What did I say?" When you do this, you take the responsibility for how someone else feels or thinks. You tell yourself, it's because of me… I'm not _____ (you fill in the blank) that Sally doesn't like me. Don't get confused because I used Sally. Sally could be anyone. Does this sound familiar? As you can see, a *"Whatever"* statement leads to the uglies--thoughts that are devaluing, diminishing and depressing. These thoughts take away your power and put you in a nonproductive state. You don't want to be drowning in the uglies because something negative has been spoken to you, by you or about you. When you find yourself in a place like this, you want to do something that will build you up, make you feel good and give you energy…empower you!

Here's where the *Whatsoever Principles* come in. Rather than trying to shrug off or pretend you weren't affected by a negative remark, the *Whatsoever Principles* will help you to be empowered by guarding your mind. Look at Philippians 4:8. Here you find the guidelines for guarding your mind against the uglies. If you want to think on something, think on these things: Whatsoever things are:

- True – *real; correct*
- Honest - *truthful*
- Just - *fair*
- Pure - *untainted*
- Of Good Report – *positive*
- Virtuous – *honest*
- Praiseworthy – *admirable* (worthy of praise)

When you apply the *Whatsoever Principles*, you empower yourself to guard your mind and take control of your thoughts. Remember: the *Whatsoever Principles* **empower** (*give you power*), **affirm** (*establish*), and **nurture** (*take care of*) you. Take a stand today to stop allowing what anyone says or does to shape you into their mold for you. Take your power back and control your thinking and guard your most valuable beauty asset from contamination by toxic people, toxic words and toxic experiences.

Take a moment to think about this saying: *"What someone else thinks of me is none of my business."* Write what it means to you._____

_____

_____

Remember, you are more than someone else's perceptions, ideas, stereotypes, or evaluations. Unfortunately, many of you spend way too much time filling your minds with thoughts that don't empower, affirm or nurture. It's no wonder you walk around with scowls on your faces. You forget that what you see and hear affects your thinking. How you think affects your emotions, and your emotions affect your appearance and ultimately the things you do.

Thinking is something you do automatically. However, what you think is up to you. You can decide what you will allow into your mind. In order to keep the uglies from taking up residence in your mind, you will need to police (guard) your thoughts and not give in to the uglies…thoughts that are devaluing, demeaning and depressing. Decide today, right now to stop allowing the uglies to bring you down. Instead, make the effort to guard your thoughts using the *Whatsoever Principles.*

When the *Whatsoever Principles* are faithfully applied they will revolutionize your thinking. Start today to tell yourself; whatsoever things are true, honest, just, pure, of good report, virtuous and praiseworthy. Begin to tell yourself today, I am:

- *made in the image and likeness of God; (Genesis 1:27)*
- *fearfully and wonderfully made; (Psalms 139:14)*
- *a little lower than the angels; (Psalms 8:5)*
- *His (God's) workmanship, created for good works. (Ephesians 2:10)*
- *Beautiful, because God has made everything beautiful…(Ecclesiastes 3:11)*

Now close your eyes. Think on these things. "How do you feel when you think you are…fearfully and wonderfully made; God's masterpiece, unique, one of a kind, special?" Are you beginning to understand that what you think affects the way you look because what you think affects the way you feel and what you feel is recorded on your face?

How do you think you would feel and look if you could think, empowering, nurturing, affirming thoughts all the time? Impossible, you say. Not really. Just as you learned to think negative thoughts you can learn to think positive thoughts. You see, you got into a habit of thinking the way you do. Just as you formed that negative thinking habit, you can form the *Whatsoever Principles* thinking habit. You might not stop your old thinking pattern right away but, you can definitely change it. Every time an "ugly" (I can't; I'm not,) thought enters your mind, stop it. Say, ***STOP!*** (I prefer, ***CANCEL, CANCEL!***) Whichever statement you choose, make sure you say it loud and strong! (Just a note: You don't have to shout it out loud, just say it strongly in your mind.) You've got to get your mind's attention.

Next, you need to replace the **uglies** *(devaluing, demeaning, depressing thoughts)* with **whatsoever** (empowering, affirming, nurturing thoughts). Let's try it.

Sally tells you, "I don't like you because your nose is big." You turn away, roll your eyes and say "whatever." Later you think Sally doesn't like me because I've got a big nose. My nose is big…I'm ugly. **STOP!**

Take time right now to think of a time when someone said something negative to you or about you. Write down how you could use the *Whatsoever Principles* in the situation.

What does the Whatsoever Principles say: Think of those things that are **true**. *"My heavenly Father doesn't say I'm ugly. He say's I'm beautiful."* So, I'm beautiful. I'm unique, my nose is unique. I am fearfully and wonderfully made. I am God's masterpiece, created in His image." What Sally says is not true. I'm not going to let Sally's negative words cause me to think and feel bad about myself.

Change will not come overnight, (I read somewhere that for every **one** negative statement accepted, it takes **10** positive statements or more to neutralize the negative). It doesn't matter how many positive statements it takes if you will make the effort to guard your thoughts, you will be surprised how quickly you will get into the *Whatsoever Principles* habit.

Lesson Two has given you a lot to think about. You were given the opportunity to study your facial features and then discussed how you feel about the way you look. Later, in the chapter, you discovered the *uglies* and how the wrong thoughts can affect your looks. Then, you learned to apply the *Whatsoever Principles* in order to guard your thoughts and protect your most valuable beauty asset…your mind.

You know what affects the way you look now it's time to move on to another aspect of your face…your face shape. Each face is distinguished by its shape. Some shapes are round while others are square or even pear-shaped. Knowing the shape of your face is important because face shape will help you determine the hair styles you can wear that will compliment your particular face-shape. Let's begin by learning the characteristics of the different face-shapes.

The members of the God Squad will help you identify your face shape and learn to select hair styles that will complement and enhance your particular face shape.

Face Facts

Mia is our Round-Shaped Face member of the God Squad. Is your face-shape like Mia's? Look at the characteristics below to determine if you have a round face.

Characteristics of a Round Face

♥ Wide with full checks and a circular form

Goal: Elongate face

♥ Height at crown and a bare forehead will lengthen and slim face

♥ Tousled side bangs will shorten face

♥ Wearing hair close to the sides of face will have a lengthening effect

♥ Wearing a side-part will also have a lengthening effect.

• Avoid straight falling bangs.

Jade is our Pear/Triangle Face Shaped member of the God Squad. Is your face shape like Jade's? Look at the characteristics below to determine if you have a pear/triangle face.

Characteristics of a Pear-Shaped/ Triangle Face

♥ Wider jawline than forehead or wider forehead, narrow jawline

Goal: Widen forehead (pear-shaped);

Goal: Narrow jawline; narrow forehead, widen jawline (triangle)

♥ Focus on a full crown to balance jawline

♥ Keep hair at the temples full/wide

♥ For longer styles angle hair below the ear and forward toward the chin to soften and narrow the jawline

♥ Shorter styles might try tucking hair behind ear

♥ Best hair length is at the chin or longer

Christine is our Square Face Shaped member of the God Squad. Is your face-shape like Christine's? Look at the characteristics below to determine if you have a square shaped face.

Characteristics of a Square Face

- ♥ Angular jaw and/or brow, with jaw and brow being nearly the same

Goal: Soften jawline and brow and elongate face

- ♥ Height and fullness at the crown will help elongate and soften face

- ♥ Short styles should be kept round and soft

- ♥ Longer styles look well with hair swinging forward into the face to reduce angles

Angelica is our Heart-Shaped Face member of the God Squad. Is your face shape like Angelica's? Look at the characteristics below to determine if you have a heart shaped face.

Characteristics of a Heart-Shaped Face

- ♥ Wider forehead/temple/check bones than jawline

Goal: Diminish forehead width and create a wider jawline

- ♥ Side part with soft bangs swept over to one side will balance forehead width

- ♥ Best length mid-neck with fullness at the bottom

- ♥ Soft, rather than angular, styles suit this face shape particularly well

Eve is our Rectangle-Shaped Face member of the God Squad. Is your face shape like Eve's? Look at the characteristics below to determine if you have a rectangle shaped face.

Characteristics of a Rectangle Face

- ♥ Narrow from forehead to jawline

Goal: Add width to and shorten face

- ♥ Bangs help cut the length of face. (Either straight bangs that blend into the side or a sweep of hair with a low side part brushed across the forehead and secured with a comb, clip, etc.)
- ♥ Optimal hair length – mid-neck
- ♥ Opt for a side rather than center part

Sadie is our Oval-Shaped Face member of the God Squad. Is your face shape like Sadie's? Look at the characteristics below to determine if you have an oval shaped face.

Characteristics of an Oval Face

- ♥ Wide at the cheekbones/temple with the forehead and jawline tapering in at the same width

Goal: Accentuate features of choice

- ♥ May wear nearly any style – long, short, layered or one length
- ♥ Focus on the facial feature you want to emphasize or soften (Example: bangs accent the eyes.)
- ♥ **Be Creative**

Once you have identified your face shape go through your favorite magazine and find three styles you can wear that compliment your unique face shape:

In closing, remember to enjoy your uniqueness. One particular face-shape is no better than another. Each one carries with it distinctive characteristics. Some characteristics you will choose to compliment and others you will choose to minimize. However, no matter what your face shape, it is just one of the many characteristics that make you unique. You are God's masterpiece (Ephesians 2:10)…one of a kind. He didn't make a mistake when He made you. So enjoy your uniqueness!

Prayer:

Heavenly Father, thank you that I am who You say I am and not what others say or think. Thank You that I no longer allow the uglies to bring me down. Thank you for the "Whatsoever Principles". Today, Father I choose to be empowered and guard my thinking against the uglies and think on whatsoever things are true, honest, just, pure, of good report, virtuous and praiseworthy. I will no longer allow toxic people and toxic words to have a place in my heart.

Father, I pray for those that have spoken harsh and cruel words against me. I forgive them and ask that you will bless them and bring them to understand the power in their spoken words. I ask these things in the Name of Your Son, Jesus Christ. Thank You that you make my enemies to be at peace with me and that You watch over me and never, never leave me alone. Amen

Read and Commit to Memory:

Genesis 1:27; Psalms 129:14; Psalms 8:5; Ephesians 2:10

Start practicing the Daily Dozen

- I am fearfully and wonderfully made;
- I am made in the image and likeness of God;
- I am unique. There is no other like me;
- I know I'm somebody, cause God don't make no junk;
- I am capable and confident;
- I walk with my head high and my back straight.

LESSON FOUR – THE VALUE OF A WOMAN

"Everyone has the obligation to ponder well his own specific traits of character. He must also regulate them adequately and not wonder whether someone else's traits might suit him better. The more definitely a man's character is, the better it fits him."

Cicero

"Who can find a virtuous (good, righteous, moral, honest) woman, for her price is far above rubies"…
Proverbs 31:10 (KjV)

I know, you are not a woman yet but you are on your way. Each day you are growing and acquiring new information, meeting new people, reading more books and having more experiences that all contribute to the woman you will become. One very important aspect of this development is the establishing of values. According to one writer values, "are the things we do that make us feel our best or that we find attractive in ourselves. They motivate us and make our activities more satisfying. Values define who we are and when we are in touch with our values it becomes easier to make choices and decisions."

However, at this stage in your life, you are struggling with trying to find out who you are, so as you grow and mature, your value system will undergo changes. Sometimes it might appear that you run hot and cold depending on which day and what the topic is, but understand this too is a part of your development process. Even though on some days you might feel like you're worth a million bucks or on other days you wouldn't give a penny for your thoughts, you are still of infinite value.

However, right now what value (price) would you place upon yourself? There is no wrong or right answer to this question. The question is to start you to thinking about your value.

$_____

In the previous chapter, we talked about renewing your mind by taking in new information. Now that you are getting the idea of mind renewal, it is necessary for you to re-think your idea of your value.

Value is defined as *to establish worth*. **Worth** is determined by *quality and quantity*. In other words, if something were of low or high quality, either level would establish its worth. Quantity, contributes to worth based upon whether the object in demand is in abundance or scarce. Where there is something in abundance, it is not worth as much as it would be if it were scarce.

One example of this is jewels or the bling as it is referred to today. Jewels, be they diamonds, rubies, emeralds, etc. are in high demand. In an attempt to keep up with the demand and provide this product to the masses, imitation diamonds, and other man-made gems are produced. Although these imitations are in great demand and are seen everywhere, if given the opportunity, the owner of an artificial gem would gladly trade the imitation for the real thing.

Because genuine gems are hard to come by and usually the quality of the stones are far superior to anything that can be manufactured, they are worth more. Place these superior gems in the hands of a master stone cutter and the demand for and value goes up even more. Why, because of the quality of the gems.

The same could be said of a woman. Yes, there are many women on earth. Yet, women are still in high demand. Photographers, moviemakers, and modeling agencies spend untold amounts of money in pursuit of a woman that possesses certain physical characteristics. Corporations, hospitals and other businesses expend large sums of money in pursuit of women possessing certain educational training. Men the world over expend a lot of time, energy and resources courting and marrying women with the qualities they believe make for a good wife and mother.

As with all things, demand will determine quality and quantity. Today, we see many images of women broadcast to us through television, magazines, videos and books. Sometimes the images of women in our favorite magazine, video or movie are shown in very seductive and provocative poses. Other times, you will see them poised in dangerous and sometimes threatening positions or situations. Then, there are times that magazine ads show only certain parts of a woman's body. For instance, her eyes, her lips, her head without a body, her arms or even just her legs are used in selling products. This is known as **objectification**. According to an online dictionary, objectification is roughly *defined as the* *seeing and/or treating a person, usually a woman, as an object.*

The images we see of women have an impact on the way women are viewed by others. The way women are viewed and subsequently portrayed is a determining factor in the value placed upon them. Let's take a minute and discuss some of the ways women are presented today.

The Modern Miss

Go through your favorite magazine, or the next time you're watching your favorite television program pay close attention to how the woman is shown. What type of clothes is she wearing? Is she showing a lot of skin? How about make-up? Is she wearing a lot of make-up? Is she intelligent or does she make silly comments. Is she mainly concerned with her clothes, her hair and her looks? Is she intelligent? What about her attitude? Does she get her way by dominating, intimidating and manipulating others? Is she presented as a total package or does the camera focus on her eyes, her mouth, her legs or some other part of her body? As you review these images, what do you think? What can you learn from the Modern Miss? Now based upon where she is and what she is doing, what value is she demonstrating? Now compare her with what you learned about jewels. Do you think she would be in the quality or quantity group? _____.

Now that you've had a chance to view the Modern Miss, write a description of her. Next, write a short paragraph stating what you think some of her *values* might be. *For instance: She is wearing sexy clothes and posing in a sexy manner,* **it appears she values being sexy.**

_____

_____

_____

_____

_____

_____

Now that we have completed the first part of the exercise, let's take a look at another image of a woman. She is found in Proverbs 31. I know she is older than you, but think about what you can learn from her. She is described as:

- Rising early to tend her household
- Her husband loves and trusts her

- He knows she won't flirt or go out with other men

- She is respected among her colleagues and peers

- She is a wise businesswoman

- Her husband and children are always nicely dressed

- Her children love her and call her *blessed (happy and worthy of divine favor)*.

Now based upon where she is and what she is doing, what value is she demonstrating? Next compare her with what you learned about jewels. Do you think she would be in the quality or quantity group? _____

_____.

Using the description given of the Proverbs Woman; write down what you think some of her values might be. *For instance because she rises early to take care of her household,* **she appears to value her home**.

_____

_____

_____

_____

There is a lot we could say about these two very different images of women, the Modern Miss and the Proverbs Woman. Each is the opposite of the other and is an example of what type of woman you can be. Maybe you find yourself drawn to some of the qualities of the Modern Miss and the Proverbs Woman. Let's do an exercise.

What do you like about the Modern Miss? _____

_____

_____

What do you like about the Proverbs Woman? _____

_____

_____

_____

_____

Now complete the following statement: If I had the things I like best about the Modern Miss, I would be _____

_____

_____

_____

If I had the things I like best about the Proverbs Woman, I would be _____

_____

_____

_____

As you complete these exercises remember the values you placed on each woman are your values. Values are what you consider to be important. Values are the foundation upon which you will make your decisions and live your life. What you *stand* for will be decided based upon your values. It's your choice; will you be a young *Woman of Quantity* or a young *Woman of Quality*?

Read: Proverbs 31

Prayer:

Heavenly Father, I thank you that my mind is being renewed and I am no longer conforming to the world standards. Thank you for showing me that I am of infinite value to you. Thank you that I am learning to be a Young Woman of Quality; standing for what I believe in and not falling for the tricks and traps that have been set for me.   Amen

Think About This:

The National Institute of Health (NIH) reported in 2003 that the Add Health Survey revealed that *"religion reduces the likelihood of adolescents engaging in early sex by shaping their attitudes and beliefs about sexual activity."*

The survey further showed that 98% of teens said it was important to be a person of good character; however, 62% of the same teens said they cheated on a test, 82% said they had lied to a parent about something significant, and 27% had stolen something from a store, all within the last 12 months.

Growing up and discovering who you are can be like going through a maze; however, remember God made you and He knows the plans He has for you. Stay on the path He has set for you. Then, you can go confidently into your future knowing your steps are ordered!

"You will be a crown of splendor in the LORD's hand, a royal diadem in the hand of your God." (Isaiah 62:3)

Darlene Laney

Did you know you are a jewel? Well you are and the month you were born is repesented by a particular gem stone. Find your birthstone below:

January	-	Garnet	July	-	Ruby
February	-	Amethyst	August	-	Peridot
March	-	Aquamarine	September	-	Sapphire
April	-	Diamond	October	-	Opal
May	-	Emerald	November	-	Topaz
June	-	Pearls	December	-	Turquoise

42

LESSON FIVE – STANDING, SITTING AND WALKING

(If You Don't Stand for Something, You Will Fall for Anything - Barb Alexander)

"To be yourself in a world that is constantly trying to make you something else is the greatest accomplishment."

Ralph Waldo Emerson

You might be asking yourself, "What difference does it make how I stand, sit or walk?" Well, did you know that the way you stand, sit, and *yes* even walk gives others an indication of the way you feel about yourself. The way you walk can tell a person if you are happy or sad. In fact, research shows that the way you "carry" yourself can be an indicator of whether or not you will become a victim.

Another important aspect of the way you carry yourself is how you feel about yourself. Have you ever noticed that when you feel good about yourself, everyone knows? It's that smile on your face, the sparkle in your eye, and the bounce in your step! Yes, when you feel good about yourself, it shows!

Feeling good about you involves thinking positive thoughts about yourself. When you think good thoughts, you feel good and when you feel good, you do good things. Good feelings lead to good actions. Think about it: you are somebody!

Take a minute and write down what that statement means to you

_____

_____

_____

When you feel that you are somebody, you realize that you are very important or of infinite value. The word **infinite** is defined as; *inestimable, immeasurable, unlimited*. **Value** is defined as *worth, merit, or price*. Therefore, you are of *inestimable, immeasurable, unlimited, worth, merit or price*!

A young woman that feels she is valuable has ***values*. Values** are *social principles (main beliefs), goals (aims, ambitions), or standards (ethics) held or accepted by an individual.*

Before we go any further, take a moment and write down some of your principles (main beliefs) and standards (set of guidelines)   I value honesty.

_____

_____

_____

Some of you might have responded that you value friendship because having friends is important to you. Others of you might say that you value family because blood is thicker than water. Or, maybe some of you responded that you value honesty or loyalty. However, you responded is correct. There is no right or wrong answer to this exercise. Your values are just that...your values. It's a personal thing.

Did you find it difficult to define your values? If you did take time to think about them. Values are important. Your values are the foundation upon which you will develop and build your character. You are still sorting through the many messages you are receiving and comparing them with what you already know.

At this stage of your development, I would compare you to a rosebud. Like the rosebud before it blooms into a mature rose, it is constantly absorbing nutrients. These nutrients get to the developing bud through the root system of the plant.

You too are absorbing nutrients; however your nutrient sources are quite different from the rosebud. A plant receives nutrients from its root system. You receive nutrients (*stimulus – those elements that contribute to your growth*) through what you hear, see, taste and touch.

Sometimes, the developing rosebud will be introduced to something that does not support its growth. When the rosebud finally opens the bloom is not as beautiful as it could have been had it not received toxic ingredients into its system.

This can also be true for you. Not everything that you take into your system through your senses **supports** (*nurtures, affirms and empowers*) you. In order for you to bloom into the beautiful young woman you were created to be, it is necessary that you receive the right nutrients or in this case information. As mentioned in the previous chapter, you learned the importance of guarding your mind and policing your thoughts. So too, it is important to be careful what you take into your mind (*Proverbs 4:23*).

What you think about consistently, you will become. What you become depends on what you do or the habits you form. In order to develop habits that support you, it is important that you take in those things that will add to and help you build upon becoming the young woman you were created to be.

Are You Getting the Message?

Earlier we mentioned you are receiving many **messages** (*meanings, points of view; ideas*) from different sources. Each day you are bombarded with messages about whom you are as a young woman; what you should do; how you should talk and what you should wear, etc. These messages can come from your favorite magazine, television program, videos, your friends, parents, teachers, minister, and on the list goes.

Some of these messages are in your face and others are more **subtle** (*clever, shrewd, crafty*) and difficult to understand. However, if you will take a little time, you will be able to determine the message. Are you ready for another exercise? Let's take a look at some of the messages you have been receiving from what you have read, seen or heard.

Exercise:

1) *Write down the title of your favorite book.*_____

_____

_____

*What message have you received about yourself from this book?*_____

_____

_____

2) *What is your favorite magazine?*_____

_____

_____

What message have you received about yourself from this magazine?___ _____

_____

_____

3) *Write down the title of your favorite television program.*_____

_____

_____

*What messages does this program give you about yourself?*_____

_____

_____

4) Write down the name of your best friend. _____

_____

_____

    What message does he/she give you about yourself? _____

_____

_____

5) How do the messages you receive from your favorite book, magazine and friend compare with your values? _____

_____

_____

Are you getting an idea that what you read, watch on television or listen to impacts you because what you read watch on television or listen to is sending you a message about you. The messages you receive from these sources helps to shape you into the person you will be in the future. (Read Proverbs 4:23)

This exercise was presented to allow you an opportunity to review what messages you are allowing to form and shape you. As a growing and developing young woman, it is important that you receive as many positive; nurturing, affirming, and empowering messages that will contribute to your endeavor to be all that you are ordained to be.

Exercise: *Find a comfortable place. Now close your eyes. See yourself the way you want to be at any time in the future (i.e., high school, college, etc.) Take some time to write down the image you have of your future self.*

_____

_____

_____

_____

Think about it, are the things you read, watch on television, and listen to helping to build you into the person you want to be--the person you see yourself becoming?

        ☐ Yes   ☐ No

Sorry, there is no middle of the road here. Either what you read, watch, or listen to helps shape you into the person you want to be or it doesn't.

Are your friends, peers and associates supporting you in becoming the person you see yourself becoming?

        ☐ Yes   ☐ No

You will either gather information that helps you to form habits that are empowering or habits that are diminishing. It depends on you. Your dreams, desires and goals will either be realized or lost based upon the information you take into your system. Like the rosebud, you will either blossom into a beautiful rose or you will become a sickly, not fully developed rose.

Whatever you want to be, whatever you want to do. It is all possible! Remember, as you think, so are you. It's up to you. Who are you going to be? When God made you, He made you fearfully and wonderfully. He gave you everything-every talent, every gift, every ability and every resource needed to be all that He created you to be. It is up to you to build upon and develop that which is residing in you.

Don't get discouraged. Remember: "You can do all things through Christ who strengthens you." (Phil. 4:13) Whatever it is that you want to be, you have what it takes. It doesn't matter what your circumstances, your national origin, how much money you have, or don't have, you can be who you want to be!

Do you want to go to college? Then go. It all starts with a dream. Oh, by the way while you're dreaming, dream big! Remember, God is a **B-I-G GOD** capable of doing

B-I-G things! Think your dream is too big. Well, think about this:

HOW DO YOU EAT AN ELEPHANT?

I know, you don't eat elephants, but if you did, how would you?

ONE BITE AT A TIME

That' right you would take it bite-by-bite or a little bit at a time. That's how you will accomplish your big dreams. A little bit at a time: Day-by-day, week-by-week, month-by-month, and year-by-year. A little here and a little there? It all begins with one step.

Write your dream down. Next make it a goal. After you've set yourself a goal, do something every day that will move you closer to achieving your goal. Read a book. Familiarize yourself with people that overcame tremendous odds to make their dreams become a reality. Cut out pictures of someone doing what you want to do. Post the picture where you can see it when you get up in the morning and before you go to bed at night. Make your dream as real as possible. Start a dream book. Spend time each day seeing yourself becoming or obtaining your goal. Don't get discouraged if your journey seems like it will take forever. Any journey begins with one step. So get to stepping!

Do you want to go to college? Set your goal: I will go to _____

College in _____ years. Next make a plan *(Proverbs 16:3)*. Write down the steps you will take to accomplish your goal. For instance, I will meet with my counselor to determine the classes I need to prepare for college. Now work your plan. Take one step then another then another. Before you know it, you will be in college. You will be and do what you thought you could.

The way I see it, it takes just as much time to achieve your goals as it does not to. Example, if you plan to attend college in_____years; what year will it be?_____
_____. If you don't attend college, what year will it be?
_____.

Think About It!

What are you doing each day to build on your dreams? Are the things that you are doing putting you in a position to achieve the goals you have set for yourself? In other words, are your sitting pretty, or are you involving yourself in activities that are diminishing, devaluating and depressing (sitting duck)?

There's only two ways you can sit: you are either sitting pretty or you are a sitting duck. What is the difference? Well, when you are sitting pretty, you have purpose and direction. You have a plan! Someone else is not dictating to you what and how you should live your life. When you are sitting pretty, your friends, peers, and associates, will not be able to persuade you to do those things that you know will keep you from reaching your goals. (Who won't be persuaded?) You won't be persuaded! You won't be likely to ditch class when you know that every time you ditch, you put yourself that much further away from achieving your goals and realizing your dreams. When you're sitting pretty, you know what you want and you're going after it! (*Proverbs 3:26*)

On the other hand, you can choose to be a sitting duck. You can be beautiful, wear the finest clothes, live in the biggest house and be the most popular girl at school and still be a sitting duck. What characterizes a sitting duck? Well, have you ever seen that cartoon where the duck is in the middle of the pond, just kind of meandering along, unaware of what is going on around him (in this case her)? There she sits, unaware that it's hunting season and she's open to danger and any hunter that comes along…a prime target (*Proverbs 11:22*).

That's the way you will be if you don't establish values and live by them. Open to every "hunter" that comes along. Open to the many snares and traps that are set for young women today. (Can you think of some of the snares and traps?)

Wouldn't you rather be sitting pretty than a sitting duck? Don't sell yourself short. Don't be afraid to let your light shine and stand out and stand up for what you believe. No matter what others are doing around you, have the courage to be the unique creature God has created you to be. You be the *somebody* that He made you. You dare to take a stand! You dare to light up the place!

Have you heard the old saying, "birds of a feather, flock together?" If you haven't, take a look at a flock of birds the next chance you get. You will notice that they all look alike and they all do the same thing. Tell me something, if you are unique and there is only one like you, what are you doing flocking with birds? Seems to me a creature made in the image and likeness of God is out of place flocking (hanging around) with birds.

Think about it. What will you do? Will you stand for what you believe in (your values) or will you fall for anything? Will you begin to walk on the path that leads you to be all God wants you to be?

Read: *Psalms 1:1; Psalms 18:35; Psalms 33:11; Psalms 37:23; Psalms 119:133; Proverbs 16:9*

Prayer:

Thank you Heavenly Father for being so mindful of me. Thank you that I can do all things through Christ that strengthens me. Thank you Lord that I stand for something and don't fall for the snares and traps set for me. I thank you Father that I walk with sure steps because my steps are ordered in your Word. Thank you Lord!

♥ Get Creative

Exercise: Personal Collage

Instructions: On a large sheet of construction paper (color of choice) cut out pictures, words, etc. from magazines that best describe you. *(Be prepared at the next session to discuss)*

♥ Start your *Dream Book*

Instructions:

1. Get a regular composition book and decorate the cover any way you want. Use pictures, letters, colored pens and markers. Make it brilliant, and bold…like your dreams. Now, as you

2. Go through some of your old magazines and cut out pictures that reflect what you want to be, what you want to do and what you want to have in the future. For instance, if you dream of graduating from college…go through magazines and select a picture of a college graduate. Paste it in your book.

3. Under the picture write a brief statement of what the picture means to you. Example: I want to go to college when I graduate from high school.

Setting Goals and Making Plans (*"A **man's heart** plans **his way**, but the Lord **directs his** steps.)" (Proverbs 16:9)*

♥ **Set three goals**

- Write your goals on the *Goal Sheet.*

- Post your goals where you will see them every day!

Once you have established your goals take time and develop a *Plan of Action.* A plan of action will help you get to where you want to go without a lot of distractions. Remember: *If you don't have a plan, you are apt to become a part of someone else's plans.*

Chapter Three has given you a lot to think about. You might want to review this chapter before going on to Chapter Four. You've been challenged to stand for something, so you don't fall for anything, and to learn to sit pretty and not be a sitting duck. You learned that when you sit pretty, you have values and you don't allow anyone to pull you away from what you believe. You learned also, that when you're sitting pretty, you have "dreams" and you've written your dreams down in your *Dream Book.* That's not all, you also have written down your goals and you even have a plan of action that you will look at everyday because you've posted it in your room where you can see it before you go to bed and when you get up in the morning.

You're on your way to stepping out. However, before you get going, here are a few tips for learning to stand for something, not falling for anything; walking with your head high and back straight knowing that your steps are sure.

Devotional

"For the entire law is fulfilled in keeping this one command: "Love your neighbor as yourself." Galatians 5:14

The question is asked, "How do you get your own personal identity?" If you have ever been around someone who is conceited, arrogant or self-righteous, you probably realize these are not the kinds of *identities* you want to portray. And, while good grooming, wearing nice clothes and being as attractive as possible help, they aren't the basis for true inner confidence and a healthy self-image. Consult the owner's manual…the Bible.

Affirm: *I love my neighbor as myself*

Standing, Sitting and Walking

FO	THI	NG		AN	FOR	AND	YTH	F A
DO	.	IF		ST	OME	N` T	ING	R S
ILL	LL	YOU		YO	U W			

Unscramble the tiles to reveal a message. (Answer at back of book).

♥ **Proper Posture!**

Mirror Test

Stand in front of a full-length mirror and study yourself—how you move, how you stand up, and how you sit to see how you unconsciously carry your body.

While observing your reflection in the mirror, ask yourself for the following questions:

1. Are my shoulders relaxed and level?
2. Are my hips level?
3. Do my kneecaps face the front?
4. Are my feet facing front so that my ankles are straight?

Turn to the side

1. Is your head slumped forwards or backwards?
2. Are your shoulders in line with your ears?
3. Is there a slight forward curve to your lower back?

If you find yourself saying yes to most of the questions, then you surely need a few pointers in correcting your posture.

Good Posture Wall Check

Another way to check your posture is to stand with the back of your head and your buttocks touching the wall. While in this position, do not push your heels back and stand as naturally as you would.

Check the space between your lower back and the wall, and between your neck and the wall. A space of at least one inch or two in your lower back and two inches at the neck indicates you have good posture. Anything else indicates, you will have to do some work to improve your stance.

Check your posture with the examples given on the preceding pages. Remember, practice, practice, practice and before long you will be standing tall, your head held high, your back straight shining forth like the beautiful jewel you are.

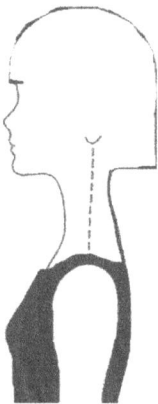

Heads Up!

1. Hold your head up straight with your chin in. Do not tilt your head forward, backward or sideways.

2. Make sure your earlobes are in line with the middle of your shoulders.

3. Keep your shoulder blades back.

STANDING TALL

The way you stand should be natural and unaffected, not haughty or pretentious.

Here are a few other tips for standing tall…

♥ Your head should be inclined slightly forward, without moving it from one side to another, or forward and backward.

♥ Arms should hang naturally at your sides.

♥ Let all the weight of the body rest on one leg, leaving the other slack.

♥ Your feet should be together, at a slightly open angle, and the knees almost together.

♥ **Practice**   ♥ **Practice**   ♥ **Practice**

Not This!

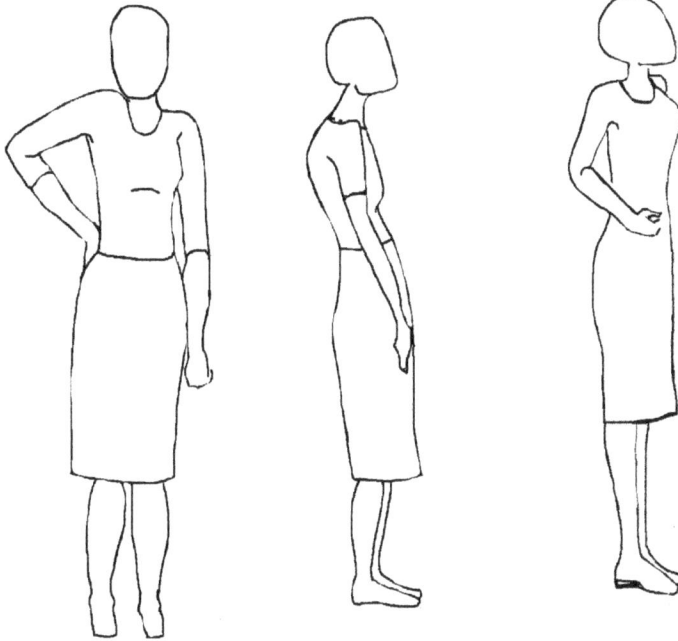

Ouch! Not only do these stances look awkward but they can be painful as well. If you identify yourself as standing like either of the illustrations above, practice standing according to the "Standing Tall" illustration above.

Sitting Pretty

How to Sit Down

Don't turn around and look at the seat before sitting. Learn to calculate the placement of the chair by backing up to it and finding it with the back of your leg. Then sit down while keeping your back straight; do not bend over. Sit first on the edge of your seat then slide back into it. Never cross your legs, never sit on your feet; never sit with your legs open. Tuck one foot behind the other at the ankle and keep your knees together.

F.Y.I.

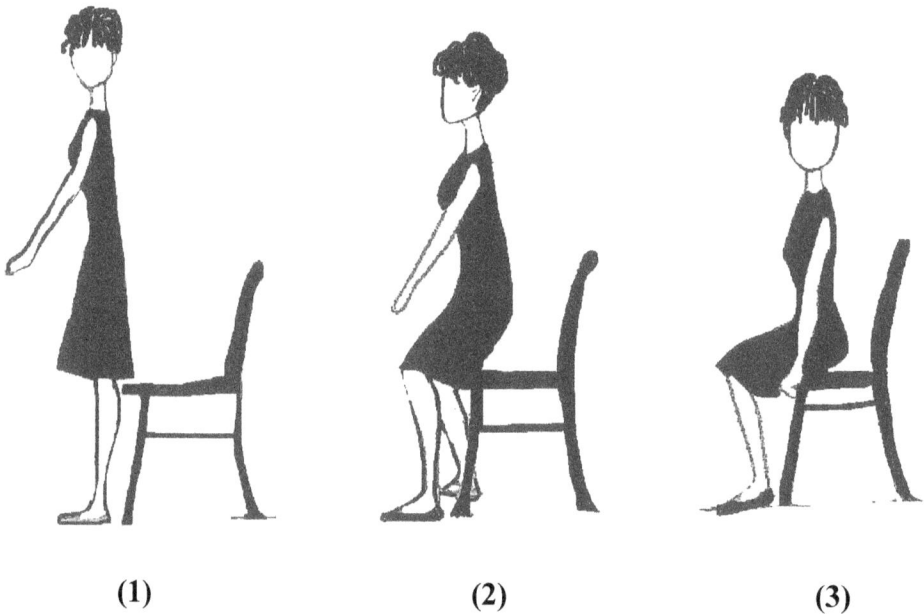

(1)   (2)   (3)

Getting back up is easier

(1)   Slide forward until you are at the edge of the seat then

(2)   Stand up straight without bending over

(3)   Don't put your weight on your hands or the armrests

OR

Will you be a SITTING DUCK?

Talk about being exposed! With today's fashions sitting like either of the illustrations, you will have far more on display than you think.

F.Y.I.

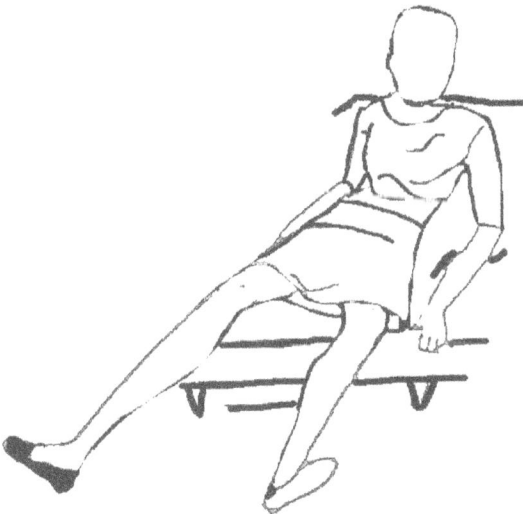

Here are a few things to remember so you won't end up a sitting duck.

♥ Don't just fall into your chair.

♥ Once seated, do not lean the body forward or slump into the chair.

♥ Don't stretch out your legs or put one foot on the other.

♥ Definitely don't sit on your hands, and finally, once seated.

♥ Don't fidget!

Will you begin to walk on the path that leads you to be all God wants you to be? (*Psalms 37:23*)

Stepping Out!

It is important to know how to walk properly. Good posture and walking go hand-in-hand.

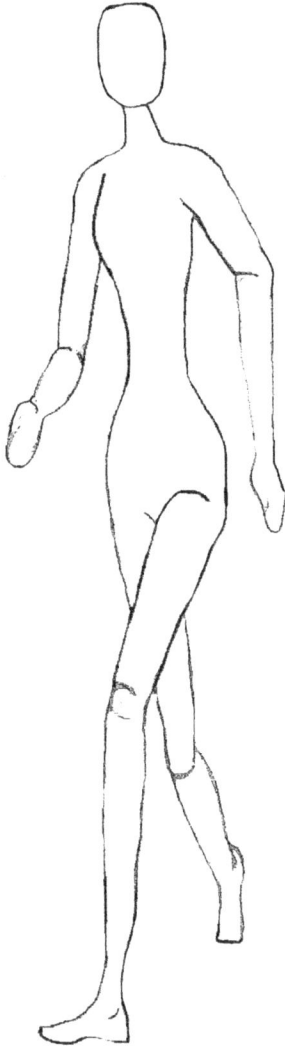

1. Keep your eyes focused forward, not up or down.

2. Chin should be pointed down and pulled in slightly, which will properly support your head.

3. Relax! Keep your shoulders back and down and relaxed. This will cause your arms to swing naturally. Do not squeeze your hands into fists, keep them relaxed. You can bend your arms at a 90 degree angle or leave them at your sides, whichever is more comfortable.

4. Your chest should be slightly lifted. Imagine that a string is attached to it and is gently pulling your chest up and out.

5. Keep your belly button gently sucked in toward your spine.

6. Use the heel-toe method. Your heel should strike the ground, then the ball of your foot and finally your toes.

7. Walk with the longest stride that feels natural. Do not take extra long strides.

8. Proper posture will help you strengthen muscles, such as your tummy, legs, and buttocks to shape and trim your body.

As you step out to fulfill your dreams here are a few tips to help you get started on your personal journey to success. Take time and review the *Success Plan*. After reviewing the Personal Success Plan, you will be ready to set three goals. Remember, your goals are your own. So, dream BIG!

4 Steps to Success – My Steps Are Sure

1. **Dream**: Start today to dream of what you want to be; to do; and to have. It all begins with a vision. The Message Bible says in part "If people can't see what God is doing, they stumble all over themselves…" (Proverbs 29:18). Make your vision as clear as you can. Read a book related to what you want to do. Start a dream book. Paste pictures that relate to what you want to be, what you want to do, or what you want to have in your

book. Remember what Emerson said, "A mind once stretched by a new idea never regains its original dimensions."

2. **Pray**. Take your vision to God in prayer. Seek his direction and guidance. Proverbs 16:9 says, "*A man's heart diveseth his way; but the Lord directs his steps*." You definitely want God to direct your steps, so remember, pray.   Pray, when things are going good. Pray, when things are rough. Just remember to pray!

3. **Visualize**. See yourself, being, having and doing the things you dream about. Refer to your Dream Book often. See yourself graduating from high school with a 4.0 grade point average. See the proud looks on the faces of your parents and friends at your graduation. The more details you add, the more real your dream becomes.

Set goals for yourself. No matter how big the dream, it can be accomplished. Remember, the elephant? One bite at a time! That is how you will fulfill your dreams, one step at a time. Goals will help you to break your dream into do-able parts. Step by step, life's a cinch; yard by yard, it's mighty hard. So set yourself some goals.

4. **Actualize**. A journey of 1,000 miles begins with but one step. So, start stepping one step at a time. Its okay if you aren't perfect and you stumble and fall. Pick yourself back up and start again. Every time you fall down that's an opportunity to begin anew. Your steps are ordered by the Lord (Psalms 37:23-24) so work your plan!

MY PERSONAL SUCESS PLAN

1. Evaluate My Situation *(Proverbs 16:9*)

2. Set My Goals *(Habakkuk 2:3)*

3. Evaluate My Goals *(Proverbs 16:9)*

4. Develop A Plan of Action *(Proverbs 21:5)*

5. Practice My Plan *(Psalms 37:23-24)*

6. Affirm/Visualize My Success *(Joshua 1:9)*

Call unto me, and I will answer you, and show you great and mighty things…
Jeremiah 33:3

Now, faith is the substance of the things hoped for, the evidence of things not seen…
Hebrews 11:1

Go confidently in the direction of your dreams. Live the life you've imagined.
Henry David Thoreau

Write Your Goals Here:

LESSON SIX – CARE OF SELF

"Let no man imagine that he has no influence. Whoever he may be, and wherever he may be placed, the man who thinks becomes a light and a power."

Henry George

There is much being written these days regarding care of the self or self-esteem. However, this is not a new topic by any means. Self-esteem has been a topic of debate for many years. Some say the level of success you achieve will be determined by your level of self esteem. Others say self-esteem has nothing to do with your level of success. Then there is the perspective that self-esteem is simply arrogance and conceit. However, as you learned in the previous chapters, what you think will affect how you feel. How you feel affects what you will do. So let's take a look at "esteem."

Esteeming Oneself

Esteem means: *respect, admire, a good opinion and high regard*. You learned earlier that you are of infinite value. You also learned that something of value is to be **prized** (*appreciated or cherished*). In other words to esteem yourself means you respect, admire, have a good opinion and high regard of self.

This does not mean that you are self-centered, arrogant or have a big head. No, the right kind of confidence can only be based on true self-worth—believing you are a valuable person to be respected and loved. Without this deep sense of worth you can never be truly happy. What it means is that true self-worth comes from knowing you are fearfully and wonderfully made, you are unique, and God's workmanship. In other words, you don't make yourself small. The things you think, your actions and what you say will be evidence of your self-esteem level.

A healthy image of self says that you care and value who you are. Although there are two components to self-esteem, this lesson will focus on the care of self.

Care refers to how you *take charge of, look after, or provide for self.* The way you do these things demonstrates the degree to which you accept, like and love yourself. When you care for yourself, it shows by the thoughts you think and the things you do.

> *"A good man brings good things out of the good stored up in him, and an evil man brings evil things out of the evil stored up in him." (Matthew 12:35)*

In order to give you a better understanding of the care of self, let us begin with a brief background of how you developed your current image of self.

Who Are You?

You began forming a picture of yourself when you were just a baby. Your parents, grandparents, siblings, aunts, and uncles all contributed to the picture you developed of self. When you got older, your friends, teachers, ministers and others added their contributions to the image you were forming of self. Without giving a technical explanation, let's simply say that during your formative years (0 – 6) your parents, grandparents, siblings and those that were influential in your life during that time gave you "messages" about you. The messages they gave to you were based upon their understanding and knowledge. Their understanding and knowledge came from messages they received from their parents, grandparents, siblings, etc. These messages were repeated to you over and over. After a period of time, you accepted the message as truth (perceptions). The *truth* became a belief and what you believed to be true you acted out.

Let me add, the messages did not stop at the age of six. After that age you received many other messages from many other sources. Not only did your friends add their message but the books you read, the music you listened to, and the movies and television you watched. All of these sources either built upon the *image* given to you in your formative years or the messages helped to form another "image" of you.

Let's review. Your image of yourself came about as a result of beliefs formed about yourself. You developed your **beliefs** (*understanding and knowledge*) based upon the beliefs (understanding and knowledge) of your parents, grandparents, siblings and others. Your beliefs were formed by you in response to statements repeated over and over. After a period of time, you accepted these statements as truth. You acted upon these truths and established behaviors in line with what you believed. Remember, "As a man thinks, so is he."

Let me give you an example of how this process works. Image for a moment that from the moment you came into the world, your parents, grandparents, and siblings praised your every accomplishment. For instance when you smiled they would gush and praise you for being the smartest baby that was every born. Every accomplishment no matter how minor, they would praise you and call you a genius! Do you think this would have had an impact on the way you thought? Let me further explain how this process works by using this example. At the beginning of a school year, an enterprising principle decided to try an experiment. He brought his teachers together and gave them an overview of the incoming student body. To one teacher he enthusiastically extolled the high academic potential of her students. To another, he stressed that her students were not so smart and that she would have to work extra hard just to get them to learn the basics. What do you think happened? You're right, the teacher that had the students with high academic potential did exceptionally well and the teacher that had the students she had to "work extra hard" with did exceptionally bad. This experiment is interesting because all the students that participated had the same academic potential.

As you read this example did it bring to mind a time when you were in a classroom and the teacher seemed to have a faulty perception about you? How did it make you feel? How did you feel when you raised your hand enthusiastically to answer a question and she/he passed over you because of their faulty perception? Unfortunately, too many of you have been the recipient of negative messaging. You have formed an image of self whose foundation is built on the flawed understanding and knowledge of others. You have accepted their perceptions as truth and established behaviors accordingly.

Good, bad or indifferent, the way you think about yourself affects the quality of your life and that in turn affects the degree to which you value and care for yourself. Sadly, too many times, you will tell yourself, you can't do, can't be or can't have based upon what you believe to be true.

Before you go any further take a look at the pictures below. What do you see?

Were you able to recognize the young girl? How many of you saw the old woman? Okay, here is one more. Look at the glass below. Is the glass half full or half empty? Circle or underline your answer.

There is no right or wrong answers to the exercises above. The exercises were an example of perception. As you discovered, your perception can be completely different from the girl next to you, your friend and even that of your parents. Because the way you perceive things is **subjective** (*partial or influenced by others*) it was necessary that you have more information by which to evaluate what you saw. In the above exercise, you were able to see both faces in the sketch when you were given "new" information. The new information you received caused you to look at the picture differently. When you did, you discovered the other face. The same is true for the glass of water. When you were given new information, you saw the level of the water from a different perspective.

This same principle holds true for you. When you are introduced to new information and new sources of information, you will be able to discover you from a different perspective…a God perspective.

A New Attitude

Some of you may be thinking, "I'm having enough trouble already trying to figure me out." Why do I need any more new information? I'm already changing every day. Yes, you are! That is one of the wonderful things about being human…you can change. How? One way is by changing the way you think. Remember, as a man thinketh so is he. Let me paraphrase, as you think, so are you. I know it sounds so simple and it really is. There's just one catch. You have to really change the way you think. It is going to take time. You have to do something different. In order to do something different, you have to get some new information.

New Information

One of the main ingredients or catalysts to change is the introduction of new information. Earlier it was mentioned that you formed an image of self based upon the understanding and knowledge of your parents, peers, and others. Let's call these your old sources of information. You begin to form a picture of self long before you were able to distinguish what was true from what was not true. Without questioning, you took to be truth the information you received. However, as you matured and received new information and new experiences, you became more aware of yourself and began adding to your already formulated perceptions (*knowledge obtained through the senses)* of you and the world around you. You developed your own filters (*beliefs, attitudes and assumption*) by which you evaluated the information you received. The diagram below is used to illustrate this process.

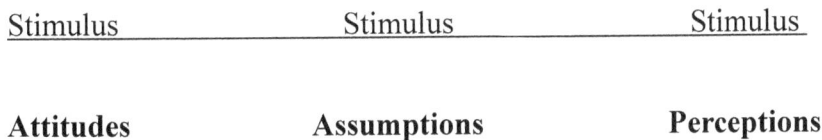

Stimulus	Stimulus	Stimulus
Attitudes	**Assumptions**	**Perceptions**

Beliefs

Because your *beliefs* were built upon information you received, in order to *change*, you will need to develop new beliefs built upon new information. You already know that some of your old sources(s) will not "change" you; therefore, you will need to seek new sources.

In seeking *new* sources of information, you will be looking for information that is: (1) **relevant** (*having significant and demonstrable bearing upon the matter at hand*); (2) **vital** (*concerned with or necessary to the maintenance of life*); and (3) **integral** (*essential to completeness*). In other words, what you are looking for is the *truth* about womankind and humankind.

I've always been told if you want to know how a thing works, consult the owner's manual. Who knows more about the product than the person who made it? Manufactures have an owner's manual with all their products because they want you to know how to properly operate their product to get the optimum performance out of it.

Think about it. Manufactures put a lot of care and attention into the owner's manual for their product even though these products will not last throughout your lifetime or into eternity. How much more your Creator has put into His owner's manual for you. He has made sure it has been preserved from the beginning of time in order that you would have the relevant, vital and integral information you need to operate at optimum performance. So get the manual out and take a look at what you need in order to "change!" By the way, in case you don't know what the manual is…it's the Bible!

A Renewed (Fresh) Mind *(Romans 12:1 & 2)*

The Message Bible tells you that the first step to *change (transformation)* is to:

> *"So here's what I want you to do, God helping you: Take your everyday, ordinary life—your sleeping, eating, going-to-work, and walking-around life—and place it before God as an offering. Embracing what God does for you is the best thing you can do for him. Don't become so well-adjusted to your culture that you fit into it without even thinking. Instead, fix your attention on God. You'll be changed from the inside out. Readily recognize what he wants from you, and quickly respond to it. Unlike the culture around you, always dragging you down to its level of immaturity, God brings the best out of you, develops well-formed maturity in you."*

Take a moment to think about this. Are you satisfied and comfortable with yourself? The person you are today is a direct result of your current thoughts (*the information you have taken in; how it shaped your perceptions which in turn contributed to your beliefs*). If you are not satisfied with who you are and the direction you are going maybe it is time for a real change.

If you have not already done so, now would be a good time for you to ask Jesus into your life. If you don't know how to go about asking Jesus into your life, turn to the end of this chapter and you will find the steps you will need to take. I pray that you will take some time and think about this very important step for your life.

The next step toward change is **not to *conform* to the world** (cosmos). I know this might be difficult for some of you but it is worth the effort to really try. Consciously make the effort to not allow what others (peers and associates) say to you or about you to "*mold and shape*" you into what they believe you to be. Remember, as mentioned earlier, you are who you are today because of your old beliefs. Your new information sources provide you with a fresh perspective of you.

The third step toward change (transformation) is to **renew your mind**. Renewal is not putting a new spin on old ideas. According to Webster's dictionary, *renewal is to make new or as if new again, to bring back into good condition, replacing what is old, worn or exhausted (tired)*. A renewed mind is refreshed; your tired thinking has been replaced with empowering, affirming and nurturing thoughts

For example have you seen an older building that has been abandoned? Looks pretty messed up doesn't it? When that building is renewed through renovation (*cleaned up, repaired or replacing worn parts*) it is being restored to its original state of grandeur. When the renovation is complete, the building is renewed! It is the same building minus all those things that made it dilapidated, tired looking and worn.

That's what mind renewal will do for you; replace your tired thinking; change (*transform*) your attitude; restore you to your original state of grandeur (*whole, complete, nothing lacking, with all sufficiency*), God's work of art *(Ephesians 2:10).*

Mind renewal is a process. As you renew your mind, you will be cleaning out the sources of old messages, stripping away your old, tired, and worn perceptions, and receiving new (relevant, vital and integral) information upon which you will make your confessions (acknowledge and declare) *(Isaiah 43:19).*

Sound complicated. It really isn't. Its three steps:

1. Take in (*new information*)
2. Take out (*old, tired and worn perceptions*)
3. Put on (*affirm – acknowledge and declare what is true*)

Reflections:

- ♥ *Belief determines view;*
- ♥ *Your current image of self is based upon early mirroring (the means whereby infants form a perception of their status, value and worth in the world);*
- ♥ *Perceptions are an individual's belief based upon their attitudes and assumptions about the situation or circumstance;*
- ♥ *Self-esteem is the personal (self) unconditional (without conditions) acceptance, valuation and respect of self, regardless of other's (parents, peers, others) opinion;*
- ♥ *You are more than the sum total of someone else's perceptions about you;*
- ♥ *You can change your self-esteem!*

Read: **Romans 12; Ephesians 2**

Prayer:

Thank you Lord that I am fearfully and wonderfully made. (Now in your own words write a prayer).

Practice the Daily Dozen:

- ♥ *My steps are sure;*
- ♥ *I stand for something; therefore, I don't fall for anything;*
- ♥ *I take care of myself;*
- ♥ *I think and say things that empower, nurture and affirm me;*
- ♥ *I am a young woman of quality;*
- ♥ *I love me, I love being me.*

To Accept Jesus Into Your Life

Congratulations on your decision to accept Jesus into your life. The most important decision you will ever make in life is to make peace with God by receiving Jesus Christ as your Lord and Savior. You can know that all of your sins are forgiven. And that you are now a new creature! Romans 10:9 says: If you will confess with your mouth the Lord Jesus and shall believe in your heart that God raised him from the dead, you shall be saved.

Prayer:

Father, I come before you today as humbly as I know how to receive Jesus Christ as my Lord and Savior. I believe in my heart and I confess with my mouth that Jesus Christ is the Son of God. I believe Jesus took all my sins when He went to the cross and that You raised Him from the dead. Your Word tells me that if I confess my sins, you are faithful and just to forgive me and to cleanse me from all unrighteousness. I confess all my sins, known and unknown and I ask you Father to forgive me. Thank you Father for saving me.

Other Scriptures to read: John 3:15 -18; John 6:47; John 14:6; Acts 2:21; Romans 5:8; Romans 6:23; Romans 3:23-26; II Corinthian 5:17; Ephesians 2:8-9; Philippians 2:9-11; 1 Timothy 2:3-5.

(Now, if you are not already a member of a Bible believing church, find one and begin to attend regularly. It is important that you be around believers because they will help you grow in your newfound faith!)

I would love to hear from you regarding your decision to accept Jesus as your Savior and letting Him be Lord of your life! Send me an email through the GSF website *at godspecialforces@inbox.com .*

Happy, happy! Joy, joy!

"Now we look inside, and what we see is that anyone united with the Messiah gets a fresh start, is created new. The old life is gone; a new life blossoms! Look at it! All this comes from the God who settled the relationship between us and him, and then called us to settle our relationships with each other. God put the world square with himself through the Messiah, giving the world a fresh start by offering forgiveness of sins. God has given us the task of telling everyone what he is doing. We're Christ's representatives..." II Corinthians 5:17-20 (Message Bible)

As you spend time reflecting on this passage of scripture from the Bible, take time and write your "salvation experience."

Affirm: I am a new person in Christ. My old life is gone!

Here's a fun quiz to take that will give you an idea of your Esteem Level. Be very honest. This is for you only. Complete it on your own or if you have a friend that you really trust, you may complete it with her. Instructions: Put an (*) next to each thought below that you've had for more than two seconds. Even if you don't believe the thought, if it nags you sometimes give it a star. Remember, there is no right or wrong answers. No good or bad. Complete the quiz in its entirety, and then turn to the back of the book for the answer key.

Esteeming Yourself

_____ I'm fat.

_____ I'm ugly.

_____ I don't look that bad except for my _____.

_____ I'm too tall (or short).

_____ I have my father's_____ (ex: nose, etc.) which is not good.

_____ I want to look like a star (model, singer, actress…).

_____ I'll never look like a star, which is depressing.

_____ Some people tell me I'm pretty, but I don't believe them.

_____ I don't do that much to look prettier, because it isn't gonna help.

_____ I wish I were cuter, so I'd have more friends.

_____ I don't care about my appearance. I'm not the girly girl type.

_____ It drives me nuts to have to wear _____ (glasses, braces, school uniform). They make me look dorky.

Count your stars and put your number here: _____

LESSON SEVEN – SKIN CARE

Did you know…
Skin is the largest organ of your body?

You've learned a great deal about valuing and caring for yourself from the previous chapters. You've learned that you are a young woman of quality as well as learning how to stand with your head high and back straight. You now know the difference between a sitting duck and sitting pretty and you are practicing to be sitting pretty. You've learned how to care for yourself on the inside. In this chapter, you will learn how to make the outside as beautiful as the inside starting with the largest organ of your body…the skin!

The Skin

The skin is the largest organ of the body; yet most young women don't do enough to maintain the skin's health. Today, American women spend millions of dollars on body products every month, but are they buying the right ones? How much do you really know about what your skin needs, what type of skin you have, what kind of soaps and lotions are the best for your skin?

One of your skin's functions is to eliminate a portion of the body's waste products through sweating. If toxins escape through the skin they disrupt the skin's health integrity.

This is one of the key factors behind many skin disorders including acne. The skin also *breathes*. If the pores become clogged, the microbes that are involved in causing acne flourish.

Great looking skin is a wonderful thing to have. However, in order to have and maintain great looking skin, you must be diligent in taking care of your skin. Not all skin types are the same. If you're in your teens, you are just at the right time to start taking care of your face properly. This will help avoid skin care problems caused by improper habits. It doesn't take a lot of time, and it doesn't have to cost a lot of money. Remember your teen skin care differs from your mom's skin care, so don't rely on her facial cleansers and moisturizers which most likely are not meant for your skin type.

By following the skin care tips for teens, you'll see what you need to do, and what you need to know when it comes to proper skin care. If you need more suggestions you can go online and find numerous sites offering advice; however, I caution you to stick with familiar product sites that make products for tween and teen skin.

Four Basic Skin Types

The four types of skin are Normal, Oily, Dry and Combination. They are determined according to the degree of oiliness or dryness of the skin. Generally, skin type correlates with pore size. For each type, a different skin care regimen is needed. Skin types also change over time, skin that may have been combination normal/oily may become more normal or dry as the skin ages. Changes in skin require that you adjust your skin care routine in order to maintain a healthy clear complexion.

Normal Skin ♥ Equal balance of water and oil. ♥ Pores are medium-size. ♥ Skin will spring back to normal when pulled away from the bony structure.	**Dry Skin** ♥ Will have a rough texture and may become flaky. ♥ Pores tend to be smaller because less oil is produced. ♥ Dry skin can easily become chapped.
Oily Skin ♥ Skin has a course texture. ♥ Pores tend to be larger. ♥ Often, girls with oily skin have a tendency to develop acne. ♥ Oily areas tend to shine. ♥ The dead skin cells may darken with exposure to the air forming blackheads.	**Combination Skin** ♥ A mixture of dry and oily areas of differing degrees. ♥ Usually the T-zone- the forehead, nose and chin – is prone to oiliness, whereas, the cheeks and neck tend to be dry.

To determine your own skin type, wash your face and wait 20 minutes. Now, pat a single piece of tissue paper against each area of your face, forehead, nose, chin, cheeks. Your oily areas will leave oil on the tissue paper.

Here are a few tips you can use in caring for your particular skin type:

Oily Skin Care:

- ♥ Remember, oily skin tends to attract more dirt and dust than dry skin.
- ♥ Your skin will benefit from soap and water.
- ♥ Washing with a cleansing bar is ideal.
- ♥ Use warm water to loosen the dirt, and then use cold water to rinse.
- ♥ Use toners and astringents containing alcohol and always use a light, non-greasy liquid cleanser.

Dry Skin Care:

- ♥ Always use mild, alcohol-free makeup and toner and a rich creamy cleanser.
- ♥ Moisturize your face every day, including the throat and the skin around your eyes.
- ♥ When you wash your face, use a liquid or a cleansing bar.
- ♥ Use warm water to lather and rinse with cold water.

Combination Skin Care:

- ♥ To care for combination skin it is ideal that you have two products, one for the oily areas and one for the dry areas.
- ♥ There are cleansers on the market designed for combination skin.
- ♥ When using these products, use the cleanser for the central oily part of the skin and dilute with water for the drier areas. To find the right combination for your skin, you might find it helpful to experiment a bit.

Remember, no matter how young or how old it is never too early or too late to start on good skin care. Start today to begin your good skin care regimen. Provided below are examples of a basic skin care regime. Remember, these are just suggestions. Should your skin be overly sensitive or is prone to breakouts consult a dermatologist.

Basic Morning Skin Care

Wash

- ♥ Use a mild facial wash with tepid water. (For oily-breakout skin, try a salicylic wash. And for normal and dry skins, try a milky cleanser.)
- ♥ Gently wash face with fingers using a circular motion.
- ♥ Rinse thoroughly (at least 10 - 15 times).
- ♥ Glide a dampened soft pad over the skin to check for any leftover impurities or residue.
- ♥ Blot dry with a soft fluffy towel. (Avoid rubbing or pulling on the face.)

Rinse

- ♥ While the pores are still open, apply an alcohol-free toner to entire face. This will re-establish PH balance and close the pores.

Night Time Skin Care

- ♥ Follow Washing instructions as described in **Morning Skin Care**.

Facial Mask (for girls 15 or over)

- ♥ After cleansing, sit with your face over a bowl of hot water to open the pores.
- ♥ Apply the appropriate mask (for oily skin choose a clarifying clay mask that draws up impurities and oils; a rutin azulen mask will help soothe and calm sensitive skin, while an AHA, antioxidant, or hydrating mask will benefit normal dry or damaged skin.
- ♥ Follow directions for time and removal of mask.
- ♥ Thoroughly rinse mask from face.
- ♥ Follow all mask treatments with a moisturizer.

Here are a few other tips to consider for healthy glowing skin:

1. Drink plenty of fluid. Water, juice, and herbal tea are highly recommended.
2. Use a sunscreen. SPF 15 is recommended. It doesn't matter if you're fair or dark

skinned, you need a sunscreen.

3. Hands off. Your hands come in contact with many different things throughout the day that are full of bacteria and chemicals.

4. Don't use soap.

5. Watch what you eat.

6. If you have trouble in the T-zone use a head band to pull hair back from the face.

Exercise: Determine your skin type. Plan a daily cleansing program for your skin type.

Skin Type: _____

Daily Cleansing Program:

A.M.

_____

P.M.

_____

Fresh and Clean – Basic Hygiene

Skin care doesn't stop with the face. Skin care takes in the whole body. Therefore, it is important that you include a bath or shower into your daily skin care routine.

During puberty your glands are more active. This is a time that you are growing faster than at any time during your life with the exception of infancy. Sweat produced by glands under the arms and in the genital area develops an order when it mixes with the bacteria on the skin.

In order to have a fresh and clean smell you will need to:

1. Shower or bathe daily;

2. Use a deodorant or antiperspirant;

3. Use a lotion or oil to moisturize skin after bathing;

4. *Optional although not recommended*: apply body powder or after shower splash.

To Shave or Not to Shave

As with everything about puberty, some girls have more hair than others. And, some will opt to shave or not. It is up to you and your mother. This is a good time to talk with your mother. She can be a valuable resource in helping you determine whether you will shave your legs and/or underarms. After consulting with your mother and you make the decision to shave here are a few things to consider.

Razor

If you're shaving your legs for the first time, be sure to use a **new razor**. A dull razor could irritate or infect your skin. There are many different types of razors available so ask your mother or if you have an older sister to go to the drug store with you to select a razor.

Remember, it is a good rule of thumb to not use anyone else's razor or allow anyone to use your razor.

Shaving Tips

When shaving your legs be sure to lather them with shaving gel. (Don't skimp on this because doing so could lead to nicks and cuts.) Gently glide your razor up your leg, in the opposite direction of hair's growth, but be careful when shaving your knees and ankles. Don't press down too hard, you could cut yourself. Rinse the razor well and let it air dry for the next time you use it.

Hand Care Tips

Your hands are into a lot of things throughout the day so it is important for you to wash your hands! Hand washing is one of the greatest defenses against the spread of disease and germs. Wash your hands when the following applies:

- ♥ Following the use of the commode.
- ♥ After handling other bodily secretions.
- ♥ Contact with rubbish/waste bins.
- ♥ Before and after food preparation.
- ♥ After coming in contact with animals.
- ♥ After being in contact with an individual who has a cough or cold.
- ♥ After caring for a person that is ill, changing dressings, administering medicine.
- ♥ Caring for the elderly.
- ♥ Changing an infant's diaper.
- ♥ Before and after your duties if you are a food handler or health professional.
- ♥ Before changing contact lenses.

Taking proper care of your hands is very important beauty wise as well as health wise. Your hands are one of your greatest possessions and they are one of the first things people will notice.

Here are some additional tips to help you keep your hands looking good and feeling good!

1. Wash our hands before every meal and moisturize often. Choose an intensive hand moisturizer if your skin is very dry.

2. Protect your hands while you are doing household chores or using harmful chemicals by wearing rubber gloves.

3. Remember when it is cold, cold wind can strip the moisture from your hands. So, it is necessary to protect them by wearing gloves. If you forget your gloves, you can still protect your hands by putting them in your pockets or by pulling your sleeves to cover your hands.

While we are on the topic of hand care it is important to mention there are some things your hands should not touch! You have been going through the workbook and learning new and productive habits that will help you become all you were meant to be. So, watch out that you don't handle cigarettes, alcohol or other substances that will not only detract from your beauty but are a threat to your health and well-being. Don't Forget...

JUST SAY NO!

If you want to really soften your hands; just before going to bed try slathering your hands with a rich creamy lotion. Put on gloves. Keep on all night. Remove in the morning and enjoy you soft hands.

Make-Up...

Before we leave this chapter let's talk a little bit about make-up. Make-up is one of those conversations you need to have with your mother. If, and when you do start wearing make-up, I highly recommend that you check out Donna Fujii's website at: www. donnafujii.com. Take the short color analysis test to determine your best make-up colors. Colors that accentuate not over-emphasize!

As a teenager you can experiment with makeup by starting with a simple lip gloss, mascara and blush, slowly adding to the makeup collection as you get older. Keep your make-up simple avoiding foundation and harsh black eyeliner. For more tips on make-up for teenagers go to www.freemakeuptips.com

One of the top natural beauty tips for teenagers is the use of water. Water is your number one beauty ally. For the teenager, water is a great help in maintaining your natural beauty. Drinking large amounts of water everyday will be helpful for the skin and your health. Most dieticians recommend that you drink at least eight, eight ounce glasses of water per day as drinking water is essential to maintain your overall health and beauty. As much as possible try to avoid drinking sodas that contain high amounts of sugar, and caffeine drinks because your skin is quite sensitive and these beverages can affect your skin's sensitive balance.

Here are some other top beauty tips for you from: http://EzineArticles.com/1490364 to make you feel naturally beautiful and gorgeous in many ways:

- Have more time to pamper oneself such as sinking into a steamy and hot scented bath. Water can help soothe and relax the muscles and mind. The steam can also help clear the open pores of the skin through deep cleansing. Deep cleansing helps improve the blood circulation of the surface of the skin and promotes the new skin cell's regeneration.

- Have a healthy diet by eating balanced foods to help improve your natural beauty as well as your figure and the body. Eating lots of fresh vegetables and fruits will result in a clear and glowing complexion.

- Taking care of the skin will help bring out your skin's natural beauty. Exfoliating regularly removes dead skin cells and replaces them with new skin cells.

Prayer: *(Exercise) Develop your own personal conversation with God.*

LESSON EIGHT – BODY CARE

Did you Know …
- *If mannequins were real women they'd be too thin to have babies;*
- *If Barbie were a real woman, she'd have to walk on all fours due to her proportions;*
- *Only ten women on the planet look like supermodels and even they need help.*

Getting Down to Basics

As a young woman, the time has come for you to take charge of the many aspects of your well being. Establishing good habits now may help you enjoy a healthier life. This means not only eating right, exercising moderately, getting adequate sleep but also keeping clean and well.

As young women, some of you are experiencing the body changes that come with the normal growth process evidenced by your development of wider hips, fuller breasts and more body fat. For those of you who have not reached this stage of development or are just entering this stage of development fear not, it is just a matter of time.

For some of you, these changes might appear distorted when compared with the image of super slim females seen in movies, television, advertisements and videos. Should you select your favorite video star, movie star, and so on, as your role model, you may find yourself confused and dissatisfied with your particular body shape.

Unfortunately, too many girls your age select these unrealistic role models. Wanting to attain the look of your favorite star, many of you are likely to reject your particular body image and strive to obtain the unrealistic image paraded before you through the media. Such efforts can lead to chronic dieting or even eating disorders.

No matter what your body shape or size, remember every body is different. "You are wonderfully made, unique, and one of a kind." Your body is just that, *your body*. It is the temple of the Holy Spirit. It is the only one you will ever get. Take care of it and treat it respectfully by giving it proper nutrition, adequate exercise, plenty of rest and keeping it clean and well groomed.

Are you ready to get down to basics? Well, let's get started. First, let's take a look at proper nutrition. Simply put, proper nutrition is putting the right fuel into your body in order to assure its optimum performance. You get fuel for your body through the food you eat.

Eating right is eating smart. Eating smart will take a little practice but is oh so worth the effort. So let's get started now.

Diet - The Food Pyramid

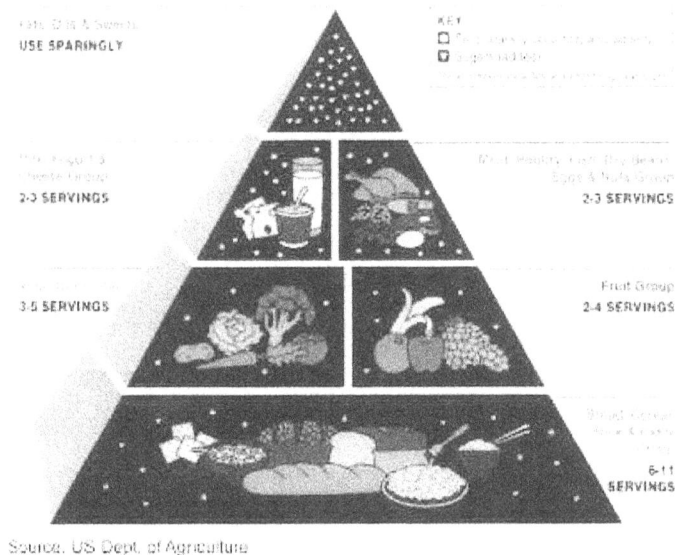

Source: US Dept. of Agriculture

Establishing good eating habits begins with knowing what to eat and how much to eat. The food pyramid is an easy way to show the groups of food that make up a good diet.

Notice, the foods that make up the base of the pyramid, the foundation, should provide the bulk (the largest part) of your diet, and as you go up the pyramid, the requirements get smaller.

As an adolescent, your nutritional needs are greater at this time than any other time in your life. Because you are still developing physically, balanced nutrition is crucial. And, because you tend to be more active, you also require more calories. The following diet plan is based on the USDA food pyramid and its specific recommendations for growing teens. Before leaving the subject of good nutrition, it is important to note the number of servings recommended for each group. However, serving size can differ for each of you based upon your eating habits. The serving sizes of the food pyramid are not so varied and require taking into consideration to be sure you do not overdo. If you are accustomed to ordering your meal super sized, you might find portion control to be challenging but take heart, just like with all the other things you have "changed," you can also change this! So let's talk about portion control.

A Word About Portion Control! (Adapted from www.pandaloveschristmas)

- ♥ One serving of meat should be the size of a deck of cards.
- ♥ One serving of cake, brownies or cookies should be the size of a post-it note.
- ♥ One serving of mayo or butter should be the size of a standard die, and the size of 3 dices for cheese.
- ♥ One serving of rice or pasta should be the size of one fist or half a baseball (size of a cupped hand).
- ♥ One serving of vegetables should be the size of two fists.
- ♥ One serving of nuts, popcorn and trail mix should be a handful.
- ♥ One serving of chips should be 10 to 15 chips.
- ♥ One serving of chocolate should be the size of a dental floss box.

Exercise: Based upon the Food Pyramid, develop a one day meal plan. Set up your paper as indicated. Allow room for each meal. Be sure to utilize the daily recommended servings for each food group. Use the space below to write out your meal plan.

My Daily Meal Plan

Breakfast	Lunch	Dinner
Snack	Snack	

Watch Out for These!

You have spent a lot of time learning about healthy things to put into your body. However, this section would not be complete without mentioning some things you need to avoid. As mentioned earlier, you learned that you are fearfully and wonderfully made. You know that this wonderful creation requires certain nutrients in order that it will perform the way God has intended. Remember, your body is sacred…

"...Or didn't you realize that your body is a sacred place, the place of the Holy Spirit? Don't you see that you can't live however you please squandering what God paid such a high price for? The physical part of you is not some piece of property belonging to the spiritual part of you. God owns the whole works. So let people see God in and through your body. (I Corinthians 6:20) The Message Bible

Watch out! Sometimes someone will try to persuade you to try things that are not healthy for your body. They might taunt you and tease you, calling you a baby, a nerd or whatever the term is today for someone that is not "with it." Don't be fooled. Whatever, the substance, be it cigarettes, alcohol, drugs, or even fad diets, as the saying goes, "Just say No!" Don't buy into the hype! Remember, you are a young woman with a purpose, a young woman of quality that stands for something and doesn't fall for anything. Remember, just say **NO** to cigarettes, alcohol, drugs, or fad diets.

Fresh and clean does not stop with a shower or bath. Don't overlook another of your most important beauty assets – your smile. But before we get into oral health care, let's talk about care of your mouth.

Nothing ruins a beautiful mouth more than spiteful, harsh, or foul words. The Bible has a lot to say about "your words." Your words can be a blessing or a curse. They can build up or they can tear down. They can bring about reconciliation or they can cause turmoil. They can bring peace or start a fight. What comes out of your mouth is more important than what you put into your mouth.

"What goes into a man's mouth does not make him 'unclean,' but what comes out of his mouth that is what makes him 'unclean'." Matthew 15:11

Don't allow yourself to get wrapped up in the habit of gossiping and mean-talking about other girls. Remember who you are...an individual miracle of God whom God has given everything you need for life and godliness. Doesn't it stand to reason that since you have everything, there is no need for you to "hate on" feel jealous or envious of someone else. Think about it. Remember the picture of the jewel in the pig's nose.

I would recommend that each of you spend time going through the Bible and familiarizing yourself with scriptures that caution you about speaking careless and idle words. Keep them handy as a reminder for the next time you are tempted to cuss, fuss or diss someone. Enough said, let's talk about oral health care.

Oral Health Care

Nothing spoils a well-groomed appearance faster than bad breath. Fresh and clean breath and well-cared teeth will add much to your image. Should you be in doubt as to how to properly care for your teeth and avoid the embarrassment of "bad" breath, follow the suggestions below:

Brushing

- Brush teeth at least twice a day;
- Be sure to brush front, sides and back teeth;
- Brush away from your gums;
- Spend at least three minutes brushing your teeth.

Toothbrush

- Be sure your toothbrush has soft bristles;
- Purchase a new toothbrush every 3 months.

Flossing

- Slip the dental floss in between each tooth and up along the gum line;
- Flossing might feel awkward the first few times but pretty soon you will be a pro; Flossing is beneficial because it gets rid of the food that is hidden where your toothbrush can't reach.

See Your Dentist

It is important that you visit the dentist at least twice a year. Besides checking for signs of cavities or gum disease, the dentist will help keep your teeth extra clean, and he or she can help you learn the best way to brush and floss.

No More Bad Breath

Dealing with bad breath is an unfortunate part of life. Fortunately, there are ways to detect it, prevent it, and even treat it.

There are many reasons for bad breath, including not brushing your teeth properly or often enough, not flossing, a build-up of plague and bacteria, decaying teeth, or a medical condition. However, most often, bad breath is caused by poor oral hygiene, that is not keeping your mouth clean.

This type of bad breath is easy to prevent. Brushing your teeth at least twice a day and flossing once a day to remove food particles left in your mouth and between your teeth will go a long way in keeping your breath fresh. Also, dentists recommend that you not only brush your teeth but your tongue as well.

Getting regular check-ups with your dentist is another way to treat bad breath. Your dentist can professionally clean your teeth and also detect the early signs of cavities, gum disease, and plaque buildup.

Our next area of care is Hair Care. Hair is very important. So important is it that if it doesn't act right, it can mess up your whole day. You've heard of it, a bad hair day. Although hair is important, it is not to be what defines you. Hair, like all other external things are to be secondary to true beauty which comes from the inside.

Don't be concerned about the outward beauty of fancy hairstyles, expensive jewelry, or beautiful clothes (I Peter 3:3) New Living Translation

Hair Care

Basic hygiene would not be complete if we didn't discuss hair care. Much has been said and written about care of the hair. However, if you will do the basics, your hair will always be clean, fresh and healthy!

1. Treat your hair gently when it's wet. Wet hair can stretch which makes it more vulnerable to breakage or cuticle damage.
2. If washing hair every day, choose a mild shampoo.
3. Choose a shampoo for your specific type of hair (straight, dry, oily curly, etc.).
4. Conditioner – choose according to your specific hair type.
5. Do not blow dry very wet hair – towel dry first.

Black Hair Care

Because African American women have different hair textures it is sometimes necessary to care for hair in a different manner. Listed below are a few recommendations, you might want to try to keep your hair clean and healthy.

1. Use a hydrating shampoo.
2. Condition your hair – use hot oil treatments or deep conditioning regularly. Also try leave-in conditioners.
3. Use a wide-toothed comb –smaller toothed combs will pull, damage, and break the hair.
4. Pick your hair products carefully – do not use petroleum products on your hair or scalp.
5. Braid or section your hair before going to bed at night to prevent tangles and

breakage. Also, try wrapping your head in a scarf to prevent damage caused by cotton pillowcases.

I know we've covered a lot in basic hygiene but there is still more to go. In order to maintain a healthy, well functioning body, it is necessary to keep it moving or exercising. So, let's get ready to "move!"

Stretching

Stretching out prior to any exercise routine is very import. It warms the muscles up and gets them ready for the exercise routine. The participants of the GSF Program are taken through a routine of stretching exercises before we begin each session. Our exercise facilitator takes the girls through various stretching movements starting with the neck and continuing with the arms, legs, calves, and finally the legs. The girls really complain about the squats but when they have to do some difficult move in the step routine, they appreciate the fact that they went through the stretching exercises.

Exercise

Exercise is important for a healthy, growing body. It will improve your strength and coordination, help you in keeping your weight controlled, and reduce stress. If you don't have a regular exercise program participating in sports is a great way to exercise and socialize. Pick an activity you enjoy and get involved! Another great exercise for keeping your body toned and in shape is to simply take a brisk, 30-minute walk each day.

Move it!

Remember to keep your body in shape you will have to "move it." If you don't have a regular exercise program that you follow here are a few other examples for getting into shape.

- Take the stairs whenever possible.
- Swim, dance and bicycle.
- Do anything to get your circulation going and help your system eliminate waste fluids and toxins and bring more vibrancy to your life and your skin.

Breathe

You breathe more than anything else. Your health suffers when you are not taking in enough fresh, oxygen filled air. So, get outside and if you can't get outside, bring the outside in by opening the window to your bedroom. If its winter, it might not be possible to do this for long periods of time but an hour will make a lot of difference.

Drink Plenty of Water

Your body is mostly made up of water. So, it makes sense that pure, clean water is essential to your body's proper functioning. I know I've mentioned this before but it bears repeating. Experts recommend that you drink at least 8 eight ounce glasses of water a day!

Relax

Believe it or not, girls your age experience stress. What with school, the pressures of homework and socializing, you might find yourself feeling frazzled and out of sorts. Take a moment to just breathe! Stress is damaging to your health and affects the way you look and feel. Be sure you are getting the proper amount of exercise and restful sleep (7 – 8 hours per night).

Here are a few things you can try to help you relax:

- Take a warm bubble bath.
- Listen to classical music.
- Try aromatherapy.
- Watch funny movies and laugh. Remember, laughter is good medicine (*Proverbs 17:22*).
- Pray. Remember to begin and end each day in prayer (*Psalms 55:17*).

Another thing to remember is: watch your attitude. An attitude of gratitude will go a long way in helping you to stay relaxed (*Psalms 35:28*). Before falling asleep each night list all the things that you are grateful for that occurred during the day. Remember, *no thing* is too small.

You are on your way. Now that you have learned to care for your body, it's time to step out and socialize. Wait, you say! You're not up on your basic etiquette. The next chapter will help you put your best foot forward in any social situation!

Prayer:

Father, I am in awe of who you have made me to be. I am fearfully and wonderfully made. I thank you for giving me to understand how special I am to You. How special you created me. Father, this day, I endeavor to take care of my body the way You would have me to. I will daily practice eating, exercising and thinking the right thoughts. I will not only watch what I put in my mouth but also what comes out of my mouth. Father, I ask you to forgive me for the things I said today that did not empower, nurture and affirm those I came in contact with.

Thank you that you have given me all things for life and godliness and I have no reason to envy or be jealous of anyone. Help me to remember that the next time I'm tempted to cuss, fuss or diss someone.
Father, I thank you that as I go to sleep this night, I reflect upon the many blessings, large and small that you have give me this day and from a grateful heart, I say, Thank You.   Amen

♥   Make a "Grateful List." Put it in your binder or somewhere you can see it often to remind you of all the good things!

LESSON NINE – ETIQUETTE 101

"Treat everyone with politeness, even those who are rude to you, not because they are nice, but because you are nice.

Unknown

Today corporations and those seeking to hire college graduates as future employees scour the colleges looking for young people that have good interpersonal skills, possess excellent verbal and written skills and are knowledgeable in their field of study. However, after spending many hours in the selection of the right person to fill the job, these same corporations find it necessary to spend additional monies in training. Included in the training is a course in proper social etiquette. What do these corporate leaders know that you need to know? Corporate executives know that persons possessing not only good interpersonal skills but having good social skills as well are an invaluable asset to their company.

A young woman that possesses the proper social skills will find herself more confident and poised no matter what social situation she finds herself. She will be able to make introductions without breaking a sweat and when she sits down to dine at a formally set table she won't be confused as to which fork to use first or even which place setting belongs to her. Once you complete Etiquette 101, you too will find that you are more confident and will be able to navigate your way through some of the most difficult social settings, including the dreaded "which fork to use" dilemma?

Getting Started

When you initially sit down at a table in any dining setting pull your chair in so you're right at the table and sit up straight. After you're seated, immediately put your napkin on your lap. Don't tuck it in your shirt. The napkin should be laid loosely on your lap so it can catch any food that may not make it in your mouth. Listed below you will find a few tips that will help you navigate your way through any formal dinner with style and grace. Ready, let's begin!

To Pray or Not to Pray *(I Corinthians 10:31)*

It's up to you. However, should you decide to pray here are some things to consider.

1. Allow for a moment of silence. If you are in a group, keep your prayer silent and don't bring unnecessary attention to yourself.

2. If all dining are Christians ask if it is okay to bless the table. If so, one person prays while the others are silent. Again, do not bring unnecessary attention to the table.

3. If you are dining with someone that is praying, don't interrupt.

Utensils

First, the general rule is to start from the outside and work your way toward the service plate (the main meal plate): soup spoon first, then fish knife and fork, then service knife and fork.

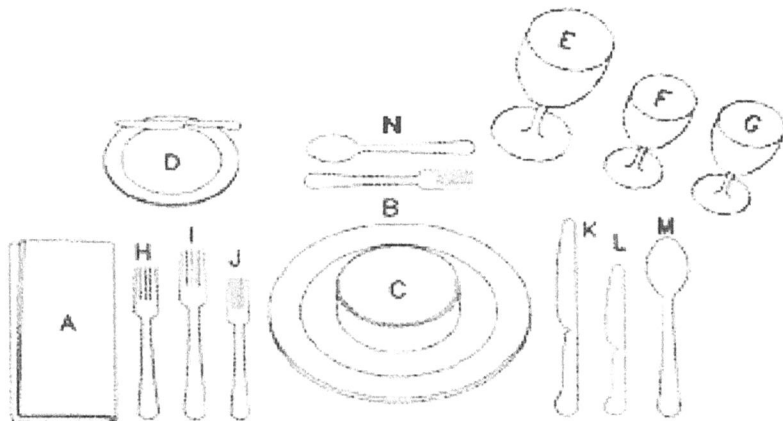

Look closely at the diagram presented. For a formal place setting, you will receive exactly as much silverware as you will need, arranged in precisely the right order. Assume the host has correctly assigned each utensil to its task. As each course is finished, the silverware will be removed with the dish, leaving you with a clean slate, all ready for the next item to arrive.

A	B	C	D
Serviette (napkin)	Service Plate	Soup bowl on Plate	Bread and butter Plate with butter knife
E	**F**	**G**	**H**
Water Glass	Wine Glass	Red Wine	Fish Fork
I	**J**	**K**	**L**
Dinner Fork	Salad Fork	Service Knife	Fish Knife
M	**N**		
Soup Spoon	Dessert Spoon And Cake Fork		

Note that it is often recommended that the salad fork (J) is placed to the left of the dinner fork (I). However, in this formal setting the dinner fork is placed to be used before the salad fork because it is suggested that the guest awaits the main meal before helping him/herself to the salad. (Taken from "Here's Information You Can Use," http://www. didyouknow.cd/info/tablesettings/htlm)

Now that you have mastered "which fork, which spoon," it is time to move on to the more challenging aspect of dining—eating.

Your food arrives, steaming hot, smelling so delicious. Your server serves you from the left. The hamburger you ordered looks like perfection itself. You're ready to dig in, but wait, everyone at your table has not been served. What do you do?

When to start eating:

Etiquette experts say if you are served first, it is okay to start eating when the meal is served hot. For cold foods or buffets, wait for the hostess to announce dinner, and wait until the head guest starts dishing.

Beginning Your Meal

Remember keep your elbows off the table, chew with your mouth closed, and do not slurp your soup or your beverage. Proper dining etiquette is important whether you're eating at a fancy restaurant or a fast food restaurant.

As you're eating, your food should be brought to your mouth. Don't lean in to the plate or shovel the food into your mouth from the plate.

Eating

The American style of eating is to hold the fork with tines facing up. Cut with the knife in your right hand and hold the food in place with the fork in the left hand. Europeans eat with the tines down. They cut and eat. The proper way to eat is to cut a few bites of food, place the knife on the plate, and then eat the bite size pieces. Always place the knife down before you take a bite.

Cutting

There are two styles for cutting: the two-step European, or Continental style and the four-step crossover American style. According to Chic Techniques, both are acceptable. However, if you're like most of us, you don't know the two-step, yet alone the 4-step method.

The Two Step Method

- Hold knife in the right hand (unless left handed, reverse these directions), fork in the left hand.
- With the tines of the fork facing down, the food is cut and the fork brought to the mouth, tines down.

The Four-Step Method

- Fork starts in the left hand, the knife in the right. Cut the main dish (steak, fish, etc.)
- Place knife on the plate.
- Switch fork to right hand and turn right side up.
- Bring food to the mouth-not mouth to the food-with right hand.

Difficult? Well, maybe at first. But, just like anything else new that you've learned with a little practice you'll be doing the two-step or the four-step in no time. Are you ready to enjoy your meal? Wait! There are a few other tips you might want to consider.

Resting Between Bites

When resting between bites, place the knife and fork, handles to the right on the plate. Never rest them on the table. When you are finished, place the utensils side by side, across the middle of the plate, handles right, to secure their removal.

Using a Napkin

When using a napkin, don't smear it across your mouth. Gently pat your mouth in a dainty sort of way.

A large dinner napkin is placed on the lap folded in half. If it is a luncheon-sized napkin, open it all the way. If you leave the table during a meal, never put your napkin on the chair. Always place it, loosely folded, to either the right or left of your plate.

Oops, What to Do?

If you've dropped or spilled something and you're at a restaurant, immediately signal a waiter and assist them in cleaning up the spill. At a fancy restaurant, the spot should be covered so you don't have to look at it throughout dinner.

If you're at a private dinner, let the host know right away and dip your napkin in your water as to make sure you don't stain the linens.

Removing inedible items from your mouth

- ♥ **Olive pits**: drop delicately into your palm before putting them onto your plate.
- ♥ **Chicken bone**: use your fork to return it to the plate.
- ♥ **Fish bones**: remove with your fingers.
- ♥ **Bigger pieces**: bigger bones or food you don't appreciate you should surreptitiously spit into your serviette (napkin), so that you can keep it out of sight.

Finger Foods

You're almost there. Just a few more suggestions and you'll be ready to dine with kings and queens, but first let's take a little time to examine *finger foods*.

- ♥ **Bread**: break slices of bread, rolls and muffins in half or into small pieces by hand before buttering.
- ♥ **Finger meals**: Follow the cue of your host. If finger meals are offered on a platter, place them on your plate before putting them into your mouth.
- ♥ **Foods meant to be eaten by hand**: corn on the cob, spareribs, lobster, clams and oysters on the half shell, chicken wings (in informal situations), sandwiches, certain fruits, olives, celery, dry cakes and cookies.

You have a few more common foods to cover and you'll be prepared no matter what is served.

Pasta

Don't you just love pasta! It's one of those foods that everybody seems to like; however, the proper way of eating pasta can be a little tricky until you learn a few secrets for getting the pasta in your mouth and not on your clothes. *Thick macaroni, lasagna* or *cannelloni* can be cut with a fork if size requires it, and any remaining sauce can be sopped up with fork-speared bread.

Spaghetti is eaten with a fork. Pick up just a few stands and twirl them on a fork. You may need the aid of a large spoon to help with the winding, but never lift the spoon from the plate. You can also have a small piece of bread handy to help keep the spaghetti on the fork if you want to avoid the spoon. Never cut spaghetti.

If your plate comes with sauce and grated cheese on top of the pasta, it can be tossed with a spoon and fork prior to eating.

Pizza

A pie-shaped wedge of pizza is held in your fingers with the sides curled up to avoid losing the filling. If the slice is large, you may eat it with a knife and fork.

How to Drink It

Drinking hot drinks from a mug is common in informal settings. A saucer may be provided underneath for you to put your teaspoon on. Most often, though, there is not one. If there are paper mats, the spoon may be placed face down on one of them, or on the edge of a butter plate or dinner plate. Don't drink from a mug with a spoon in it. You don't want to take the risk of poking yourself in the eye.

Tea bags should be placed against the edge of your saucer after the excess liquid has been squeezed out, either by pressing the bag against the side of your cup or mug with a spoon or by setting the bag in the spoon and wrapping the string around the bowl of the spoon and bag. If there isn't a saucer or plate, ask for one. Remove long-handled spoons from iced tea before drinking.

If tea spills into your saucer, ask for a new saucer. If this is inconvenient to do and paper napkins are available, use one to absorb the liquid on the saucer and let it sit there as a sponge. This is better than dripping across the table or yourself.

Paper Wrappers

If you've ever been torn between the ashtray and the floor, here's what you should really do with those little pieces of paper. Sugar wrappers can be tucked under your saucer or next to your plate, lying flat. Leave butter wrappers or jelly containers on your butter plate.

Finished

You've made it through your formal dining experience. You're finished, now what do you do? After you're finished with a course, don't place your silverware back on the table. Place them on the plate or dish that has just been used. When you're ready to get up and leave, place your napkin on your plate or to the left of your plate

Did you think there was so much involved in eating? As you can see, proper dining etiquette may be a lot different from the way you are used to eating. However, if you learn the proper techniques, you will be able to dine with poise and confidence. But, before we leave the dining experience, let me introduce you to some rules of etiquette reserved for buffet dining.

Dining etiquette for buffet dining may sound a little strange. But the fact remains that even buffet dining expects certain rules of etiquette to apply. These rules are pretty simple and are considered to be essential for a fine dining experience. These are some of the points to keep in mind, as adapted from Ezine Articles.

1. Follow the queue (line-up, arrangement)

No matter how hungry you are please maintain and follow the queue. Jumping the queue is not only inappropriate but also does not show you in good light. Also remember before you take up your place in the queue remember look to see if there is a couple or a group going before you. If so stand back and let all members of the group pass or if a couple do not stand between them. To do so is considered rude.

2. Take a plate not a platter

Yes, it is a buffet and you can eat as much as you want but it is better to go for a second helping rather than pile your plate. Don't take it all. Be careful about taking a large portion of popular food at the buffet like seafood. Take the appropriate portion so that there is enough for everyone else. Take the breads and vegetables first to ensure there is only a little space for you to take the special dish on the menu.

3. Cleanliness counts

Another thing to remember here is cleanliness. So while scooping out the portions, be careful about accidental spills. Use the appropriate dish and utensils, and bowls for the appropriate dish. Do not use serving utensils intended for a certain dish to serve other dishes. Do not mix the dishes with each other and create a mess. Also, use different plates for salads, main dishes, and every time you go for a refill. A dirty plate is not a very pleasant site with the other diners.

4. Don't overeat

Ok! You are hungry and the food is too good to resist. Still at the end of the day it is your stomach and it can digest only so much. So, even if you are tempted by the "all you can eat" offer, think about yourself and your stomach and don't overeat.

5. Don't eat while getting your food

Eating while waiting for your turn is a strict no-no. No matter how hungry you are please avoid eating while getting your food. If you are really hungry then take some salad, go to your place, and eat it so that the initial hunger subsides. Once that is done then you can go for the main course.

6. Basic courtesy

Just because you are having a meal at a buffet does not mean that you can do away with basic courtesies like saying thank you, please, and excuse me.

7. No staring, giggling or whispering

Stop! So what if the person in front of you is obese or thin like a wafer and is loading up his/her plate like he/she has not eaten in years. No matter how tempting—no staring, giggling or whispering.

Two final points and you will be ready to dine with kings and queens, or at least have dinner out and not embarrass yourself or those with you.

Excusing Yourself

When you need to get up to go to the restroom, it isn't necessary to say where you're going-a simple "Excuse me, please; I'll be right back" is sufficient. At other times, a brief explanation is in order: "Please excuse me while I check with the babysitter." Leaving without a word is considered rude.

Grooming at the Table

In most circumstances, it is more polite to excuse yourself and put on lipstick in the ladies' room than to do it at the table. The exception is when the restaurant has an informal atmosphere and you're among friends, in which case you can apply the lipstick quickly. What you should avoid is a primping routine--no compact, no powder. And then there's that never- to-be-broken rule: Whether you're a man or a woman, don't use a comb at a restaurant table, nor should you rearrange your hair or put your hands to it wherever food is served. Using dental floss at the table is a major never-ever. Believe it or not, some people have no qualms about doing something so private in public.

Wow, you did it! GSF does not expect you to master all these etiquette tips over night; however, you are expected to keep this booklet handy to refer to whenever you need to be reminded of proper dining etiquette. Let's go to the next step in proper etiquette training... introductions.

INTRODUCING YOURSELF AND OTHERS

Okay, now that you know how to navigate through a formal dinner with poise and grace, let's focus on getting through those sticky situations you find yourself in when you have to introduce yourself, someone else or a group.

Introductions can often be awkward; however, a little know-how goes a long way. There is an old saying that says, "*You never get a second chance to make a first impression.*" It's old, it's a cliché, but it's true. First impressions are lasting impressions; so, let's practice introductions to be sure we make a good first impression.

Introducing Yourself

- ♥ Smile

- ♥ If seated, stand

- ♥ Greet the other person. State your name. Always shake hands *(failure to do so implies rudeness)*. Ask if uncertain of pronunciation, or unable to clearly hear the other person's name.

- ♥ Repeat person's name. I'm glad to meet you (*person's name*) or it's good meeting you (*person's name*).

- ♥ Repeating the person's name will help you better remember the person's name.

The Art of a Proper Handshake

I call being able to give a proper handshake an art because it seems so many people have forgotten or never learned how to do so. You can learn a lot about a person by the way he/she shakes your hand. Here are a few things to remember when shaking hands:

1. As you're approaching someone, extend your right arm when you're about three feet away. Slightly angle your arm across your chest, with your thumb pointing up.

2. Lock hands, thumb joint to thumb joint. Then, firmly clasp the other person's hand – without any bone crushing or macho posturing.

3. Pump the other person's hand two to three times and let go. (Caution: be careful with this you don't want to pump too hard.)

(Handshake – Grasp hand so the webs of the thumbs meet. If wearing gloves, remove them.)

Introducing Others

- ♥ Introduce person you are least familiar with to those you are most familiar with.

- ♥ Say name (and title if appropriate) of person being introduced first, followed by name (title if appropriate) of other person. Mention both first and last names distinctly, including titles (if appropriate).

Group Introductions

- ♥ If you are making the introductions, include a bit of information about each person. This helps facilitate further conversation.

- ♥ If you forget someone's name, apologize briefly and wait for the person involved to volunteer his or her name. If the person does not volunteer their name, ask. (Example, say, I'm sorry, I forgot your name…)

First Names

The general rule for using first names is "don't" unless requested to do so.

- ♥ To a superior in one's business
- ♥ To a business client or customer
- ♥ To a person of higher rank
- ♥ To professional people offering their service
- ♥ To an older person

Use of Ms

- ♥ When introducing a woman and you are unsure of marital status, use title Ms. Not Miss or Mrs. (Mrs. – Married; Miss – Not Married)

Introducing Couples

- ♥ Mr. and Mrs. Smith
- ♥ Dr. and Mrs. Smith or Mr. and Dr. Smith
- ♥ Drs. (First Name) and (First Name) Smith
- ♥ Pastor(s) (First Name) and (First Name) Smith
- ♥ Pastor (First Name) and First Lady (First Name) Smith

Who Should Go First?

Have you ever arrived at the door at the same time as someone older than you, or someone of the opposite sex? Did you wonder which of you should be the first to enter? Below are a few tips to help you navigate these tricky situations with ease.

Male and Female

- ♥ Females should *always* be allowed to pass first. (Age is not a factor here). When a female arrives at a door the same time as a male, older or younger, the female should stand slightly to the side or slightly back to allow the male to open the door or stand back in order that the female may pass.

Female and Female (Close in Age)

- ♥ The person that is closet to the door handle should open the door and allow the other person to pass.

Older Female and Younger Female

- ♥ The younger female should open the door for the older female and allow her to pass first.
- ♥ It is also acceptable for the younger female to open the door pass through and hold the door until the older female has passed. This is recommended if the female, older or younger is carrying a package, etc.

Making a First Impression on the Telephone

Have you ever given thought to the way you answer the telephone? Did you know the way you answer a telephone tells the caller a lot about you. Telephone manners are very important. Your voice over the phone is often the first or only impression a person receives of you or the organization you represent.

Telephone Talking Tips:

- ♥ Before picking up the receiver, smile.
- ♥ End all conversations before answering the phone.
- ♥ Speak slowly and clearly into the mouthpiece. Do not chew gum, eat or drink while you are talking on the phone.
- ♥ Be friendly, but do no waste time. Get to the point of the call.
- ♥ Be a good listener and pay attention to the person on the other end of the line.
- ♥ Turn off or turn down background noise such as the radio or television.
- ♥ Remain calm during the conversation, even if the person on the other end is not.
- ♥ End the conversation with a courteous comment such as "thank you" or "good-bye." Then replace the receiver quietly.

When Answering a Call

- ♥ Try to answer the telephone by the second or third ring.
- ♥ Identify yourself (organization if appropriate).
- ♥ If the call is for someone else, politely ask who is calling, inform the caller that you will get the person requested and sit the phone down quietly.
- ♥ Locate the person requested and inform him/her of the telephone call.
- ♥ If person not available, return to the telephone and inform the caller that (person's name) is not available at this time.
- ♥ Offer to take a message.
- ♥ Take the message.
- ♥ Read information back to the caller. If unsure of the spelling of a person's name, ask caller to spell his/her name.
- ♥ Assure caller you will give (person's name) the message and end the conversation politely.
- ♥ Set the phone down lightly.

When Placing a Call

- ♥ Identify yourself.
- ♥ If you have several items to discuss, make a list beforehand so that you do not forget anything.

- ♥ Have necessary information near you.
- ♥ If the person you are calling sounds busy, ask if you can call back at a more convenient time.
- ♥ If you want your call returned, give your name, your telephone number and a time when you can be reached.
- ♥ Use available technology such as answering machines, e-mail, and faxes to leave messages.

Message Machines/Voice Mail

Message machines are one of those modern conveniences that you wonder how you ever got along without while others of you don't know what it is to be without them; however, there are a few guidelines to keep in mind:

1. Keep in mind what type of impression you want to make? Your message is a reflection of you. What a person hears gives them an impression of you.
2. Keep your message brief.
3. Do not say you are not home at this time, rather say, "I am not available to take your call at this time."
4. Consider the type of music you use. What message does it convey to the caller?

Cell Phone Etiquette

Here are a few other comments about cell phones:

- ♥ Do not subject others to your cell phone conversations.
- ♥ Do not set your ringer to play an annoying melody.
- ♥ Turn your cell phone off during public performances.
- ♥ Do not dial your cell phone while driving.
- ♥ Do not speak louder on your cell phone than you would on any other phone.
- ♥ Do not speak on your cell phone while dining with someone.
- ♥ If in a meeting and you must leave your cell phone on let those you are meeting with know this in advance.

There are many rules of etiquette that govern proper behavior in social settings, business settings as well as personal interaction. Sometimes, it can be overwhelming but with a little practice, you'll be social savvy in no time!

LESSON TEN – ACCENTUATE THE POSITIVE

"A word fitly spoken is like apples of gold in pitchers of silver."
Proverbs 25:11 (KJV)

You have spent a lot of time going through the earlier lessons learning how to become a Young Woman of Quality being trained to take your place in the large company of young women that will proclaim the good, acceptable and perfect will of God for your life. Each lesson gave you new (*relevant, vital and integral*) information that was necessary for your change (*transformation*).

Now that you have learned all this, there are still just a few more lessons. In this lesson, you will focus on accentuating or complimenting your unique features. You pretty much have it together; however, the following tips will help you learn to "Accentuate the Positive!"

FOUR PRINCIPLES FOR ACCENTUATING THE POSITIVE

REMEMBER these principles:

1. The Eye Naturally Follows Lines

If you wear up and down lines, the eye senses height and slimness. If you wear side ways lines the eye senses width and decreases in height.

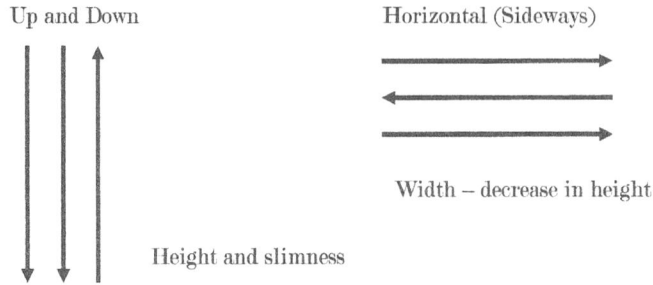

Up and Down

Horizontal (Sideways)

Width – decrease in height

Height and slimness

2. The Eye Is Attracted to Light

You minimize your proportions by careful placement of dark colors; you may accentuate your proportions by careful placement of light colors. Glossy fabrics which reflect light make you appear larger. Dull fabrics which do not reflect light make you appear smaller.

      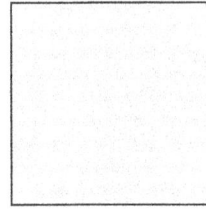

Minimize   *Maximize*   *Accentuate*

3. The Eye is Affected by Comparative Relationship

The size of accessories or fabric patterns in comparison to the total "you" is important. A tiny handbag can make a tall girl look even taller, and a bold print can swallow up a petite person, making her appear even smaller.

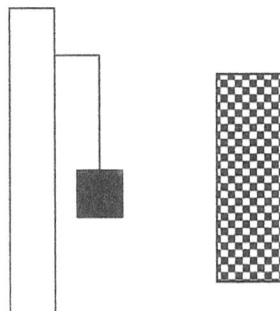

4. The Eye Responds to a Feeling of Proportion and Balance

Adding or subtracting fullness can give balance and pleasing proportion to your silhouette. For example, a full bust line will be less apparent to the eye if you add fullness below the waistline to balance your figure contour.

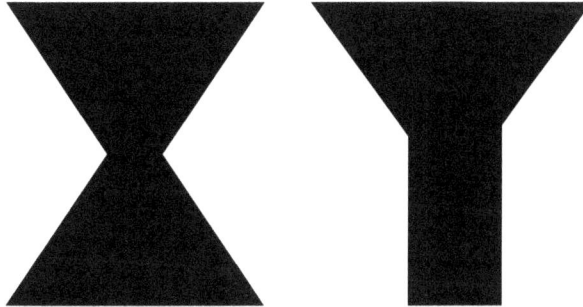

Now that you have been introduced to the four principles for accentuating the positive, let's move on to body basics.

Tween Body Basics

If you are a tween, (10-12) your true body shape has not developed yet; however, in a year or two, you will see more dramatic changes to your body as you began to take on the characteristics of one or a combination of the four basic body shapes.

Pretty Plus Figure (Hourglass)

You have an hourglass figure if...

♥ Your full hip-line and your full bust-line are the same width and your waist is well defined

♥ You most likely have a balanced body vertical body shape

Heavy at the Hip Line (Triangle)

The triangle body type is often also referred to as pear-shaped. You have this shape if...

♥ Your full bust-line is proportionally narrower than your full hip-line and you have a well defined waist

♥ You typically have narrow shoulders

♥ You most likely have a balanced body or short legged vertical body shape

♥ Your thighs are typically full

♥ You may also have a full rounded bottom

Full at the Bust (Inverted Triangle)

- ♥ You have a proportionally large bust, or you have broad shoulders, or both
- ♥ You have narrow hips with a well defined waist
- ♥ You most likely have a long legged vertical body shape with proportionally slim legs
- ♥ You may also have a flat bottom

Rectangle (Tall – long or short waist)

You have a rectangle body if...

- ♥ Your full bust-line and full hip-line are about the same width and you have little waist definition
- ♥ Your legs and arms will typically be proportionally slender
- ♥ You have a small to medium bust

This is only a brief description of body types. For more information on your particular body type and styles to wear that compliment and not over-emphasize a good site is www.dressyourbodytype.com

- ♥ **Take a moment to see how creative you are when it comes to mixing and matching**. *Answers to this quiz are at the back of the book.*

1. You have three t-shirts; pink, purple and blue. You also have two pairs of jeans; white and blue. How many different outfits can you make? (Write down your answers). _____

    _____

2. You go shopping and buy yourself a pair of black jeans and a short denim jacket. How many different outfits can you now make? _____

    _____

3. If you had two sweaters, two pairs of jeans and two skirts, how many outfits could you make? _____

    _____

I hope you enjoyed this exercise. Now, why don't you go through your closet and combine different pieces to make different outfits. I'm sure you will be surprised how many different combinations you can come up with!

Before going further, let's take time to determine your "style." Each of you has your own individual way of expressing yourself; the clothes you wear, the way you wear your hair and even your makeup. All of these in combination make up your style. Take a moment and take our "Style Quiz" to determine your style. When finished go to the answer page to identify your style.

My Style Quiz

1. **My favorite way of dressing is**

   a. Layers, ruffles and such with my own flair

   b. Classic white blouse with pleated skirt, light colored shirts with shorts

   c. Two piece sweater set with skirts or jeans

   d. Clothes that are comfortable; t-shirts and jeans even sweats

   e. Whatever the latest trend

2. **I like to wear my hair**

   a. With lots of barrettes, scrunches, flowers, and clips

   b. In a ponytail

   c. Down, with a wide headband or a pony with side part

   d. Casual, in braids, or ponytails, or up in a twist

   e. The way my favorite star wears hers

3. **Accessories that express my style are:**

   a. Lots of necklaces, the more the better

   b. Don't like a lot of accessories

   c. A single necklace or chain with a heart

   d. Colorful earrings with a matching necklace

   e. What everyone else is wearing

4. **Shoes that I like to wear are:**

   a. Shoes that let me express ME, and let me be creative

   b. Tennis shoes

   c. Mary Janes or loafers

   d. Brightly colored flip flops or sneakers

   e. The new styles of the season

5. **On Saturdays, I like to wear:**

   a. Long flowing skirts or jeans with ruffled blouses

   b. Shorts and a pastel colored T-shirt

   c. A sweater and jeans

   d. A loose t-shirt and my favorite capris

e. Anything comfortable as long as it's in style and looks good

♥ Activity: Armed with the information you have learned about body shape and style, go through your favorite magazine and select three outfits you can wear that compliment your particular body shape.

LESSON ELEVEN – PUTTING IT ALL TOGETHER!

"Plan your progress carefully; hour-by-hour, day-by-day, month-by-month. Organized activity and maintained enthusiasm are the wellsprings of your power.

Paul J. Meyer

You've invested a lot of your time and energy learning to stand, walk and sit properly. You've also learned about your face shape, how to care for your skin, good nutrition and basic exercise. You've learned based upon your body shape how to accentuate the positive. Yet, in order to maintain a well-dressed look, it is important that you spend time organizing, storing and preparing the outfits you will wear. A little preparation and advanced planning will help you keep it all together.

A Stitch in Time Saves Nine

Have you heard this saying? My grandmother used to say it to my sister and me when we were tweens. You see my sister had a habit of ripping the hem out of her skirts. Rather than take the time to fix the hem when it was barely noticeable, my sister would wait and somehow manage to end up with her hem totally ripped out. Instead of having to sew a few stitches, my sister would then have to spend a lot of time making a lot of stitches to fix the hem. Thus, "a stitch in time saves nine." I hope you will heed my grandmother's advice and take care of that small rip or hem before it becomes a big thing!

Button, Button, Who's Got the Button?

Have you ever put on your favorite jacket and go to button it up only to realize that buttons are missing: You had intended to sew the buttons on the last time you wore the jacket but somehow you forgot. Or, have you gone to button your pants or a skirt and had to use a pin because the button is missing. Taking time to sew buttons before they come off the garment is ideal. Tighten loose buttons before you hang the garment in your closet and be sure to use a thread that matches the garment. You can purchase a small sewing kit at any fabric or department store.

Fresh and Clean

Not only should you keep your body fresh and clean but it is also important that you keep your underwear and outer wear fresh and clean. It's important that you set aside one day a week to launder and iron your clothes. When washing your clothes, be sure to follow the directions for proper use of the machine as well as the amount of bleach and detergent to use. If you are running out of clean underwear and you are not able to do a full load of laundry, try hand washing your underwear. This can be done quickly and easily in the bathroom sink. Be sure to rinse your garments thoroughly. You don't want to leave any soap residue.

Neatly Pressed and Creased

Nothing spoils a look faster than an unpressed or rumpled skirt, blouse, dress, etc. Be sure you remove all wrinkles from your clothing before wearing. Even though some labels say wash-n-wear, they require a light pressing. Other clothing requires a good steam press. Read the labels of your garments for care instructions and follow the instructions carefully.

Panty Hose, Tights and Socks

I was watching a favorite program of mine and I heard the guest say that younger women are no longer wearing panty hose. I was shocked because I believe panty hose accentuate your legs and help keep everything nice and tight. However, be it panty hose, tights or socks that you wear, make sure they are clean and free of holes and runs. For that well-turned out look, be sure your leg wear matches your outfit.

Shoes

Athletic shoes, pumps, sneakers, clogs, whatever the make, color or size, be sure your shoes are clean and in good condition. If they are torn, excessively dirty, or worn over, it is time to get rid of them.

Shopping Basics

Armed with the information you have regarding your body shape and what styles compliment rather than over-emphasize, you are ready to shop successfully. However, before you hit the mall, In Style recommends that you have a plan.

In other words know what you already have and what you need. In order to know what you have, you will need to take inventory. Taking inventory simply means that you go through your closet and determine what you have that is wearable, to be donated, or needs to be discarded.

While you're going through your clothes, now is a good time to get organized and clear out your closet.

Let's Get Organized

Organization takes planning and time. Before starting, make sure you have plenty of time to finish this project. A suggestion would be start early on Saturday morning and allow at least four hours, more if your closet is in a real mess. Ready, let's begin.

Closet

1. Getting Started

Make sure you have enough hangers, cardboard boxes, clear plastic stacking boxes, and/or shoe boxes on hand.

2. Clear everything out of your closet

Lay your clothing on your bed or the floor. Try on each piece. If it fits, it can go back into the closet. This applies to your shoes also. Clothes that no longer fit or that you will not wear again should be either given away or tossed out. Apply the 6 month rule…if you haven't worn it in 6 months…toss it or give it away!

3. Putting Everything Back

Now that you have pared down your wardrobe, it's time to put everything back. Start by hanging your garments by type and color. For instance, hang all jackets together by color in a section by themselves. The same procedure would apply for your blouses, skirts and dresses.

Remember: In the summer move your heavy winter-only pieces to another closet or to the back of your closet. Do the same with your light-weight summer only things in the winter.

4. Shoes

Sort your shoes by color and style. If you do not have storage boxes for your shoes, you can line your shoes on your closet floor or on a shelf or even in the boxes they came in. Be sure to mark the boxes indicating the shoe style and color. For instance: sandal, black.

Dresser

1. It's time to get tough. Throw out all your old underwear, single as well as socks with holes, and bras that don't fit. Get rid of all of it!

2. Once you have thrown out all the old stuff, what is left is to be placed back into the dresser. Fold each item neatly and place it back into the dresser. (Tip: An inexpensive way to keep your undies smelling fresh is to tuck a fabric softener sheet into the drawer.)

Accessories

1. Go through the same process with your accessories. Arrange items neatly in a large jewelry box, clear plastic divided boxes or baskets. Belts should be hanging together or in clear boxes.

If you repeat this process every three months your closet and drawers will always be neat and orderly.

♥ Get Creative

A fun project for personalizing your closet space is to create your own accessory hanging board.

Instructions:

1. Start with a medium sized piece of wood. (You can buy this from your local craft store).

2. Cover the board in a colorful fabric.

3. Add colorful push pins and colored ribbon.

4. Attach a ribbon to the back so you can hang your board to the back of your closet door or on the wall; wherever space permits.

5. Hang your necklaces, bracelets and other accessories

6. Lastly, enjoy your creative and useful accessory hanging board.

   There are so many exciting craft ideas for personalizing your closet space. I hope you will take the time to either go on line or visit your local craft store for some fun projects. Take advantage of them. You don't have to go alone. Take a friend with you and enjoy your creative venture.

Last Word

Congratulations! You've completed the GSF Charm Course. I encourage you to continue to practice the many things that you have learned. Continue to practice walking with your head high and back straight. Don't forget to continue to sit pretty and stand for something so you don't fall for anything. Whatever, you do, don't put this book away and forget all the many things that you have learned. Keep dreaming and adding to your dream book and don't forget the "Daily Dozen." Continue to guard your thoughts so you don't become a victim of the *Uglies*. Remember it's not whatever but *whatsoever*.

You have now completed the training program that makes you a member of a very elite group of young women. You have taken your natural God-given talents and abilities and turned them into skills that will help you go forth with grace and poise proving the good, acceptable and perfect will of God for your life.

You may receive your "Certificate of Completion" by completing the request form at the end of this book. Follow the directions carefully and within two to three weeks, your Certificate will arrive in the mail for you to frame and hang on your wall.

You are now a fully trained and equipped member of...

God's Special Forces

I'm Committed

I _____ am committed to being the best that I can be.
Therefore, I commit to:

1. Participate in all activities of the GSF program.
2. Practice the exercises suggested in each lesson.
3. Pray the prayers at the end of each chapter.
4. Memorize the Scriptures suggested.
5. Give my best so that I can be my best.
6. Be myself.
7. Free myself.
8. Treat others as I want to be treated.
9. Interact with others in a respectful and gracious manner.
10. At all times act in a way that is consistent with the standards of the GSF program.

On this _____ day of _____ I give myself permission to
become a part of and enjoy the GSF experience!

Signed:

_____

Answer Page

♥ **Word Tiles (page 51)**

I Stand for Something, not Falling for Anything!

♥ **Combination of outfits (page 104)**

5 (white jeans with pink, purple and blue shirt; blue jeans with pink and blue shirt)

6 (black jeans with pink, purple and blue shirt; jacket with each)

? did not know colors, etc.

♥ **Answer Key - Esteeming Yourself (Page 67)**

♥ *If you have between 11 and 13 stars*:

You seem to be having a tough time seeing your own beauty. Sometimes we have a tendency to focus so much on the things we don't like about ourselves that we forget that we have much, much more to celebrate! Focusing on the positive will be especially amazing for you. God wants you to honor and love yourself. Keep working and you will get there!

♥ *If you have between 4 and 10 stars*:

You are not alone. Most girls your age go back and forth with their feelings about themselves. Keep learning, growing and questioning and you will get in touch with a true picture of yourself that can get better all the time.

♥ *If you have between 0 and 3 stars*:

You are in a great place to have some fun with your beauty right from the start. Pay attention to the things that you did star, those are the kind of thoughts that will keep you from shining your brightest.

♥ **Answer Key – Style Quiz (page 105)**

If you circled mostly:

A. You are **BOHO CHIC**. You are artsy and chic and like to express your unique style even though it is outside of the latest fashion trends.

B. You are **PREPPY**. You love the look of light colored shirts paired with your skinny jeans, pleated skirts and classic white shirt.

C. You are **CLASSIC**: You don't go for the latest trends. Instead you like timeless fashion designs--semi-fitted jackets; Mary Jane's or loafers and simple accessories.

D. You are **CASUAL**: Comfort is your motto. You to live your life free of the restrictions of fashion, so you avoid high heels and may not even own a dress

E. You are **TRENDY**: Bring it on--the latest, newest, cutting-edge fashion designs in both clothing and accessories. These all catch your attention. You are the one your friends are more likely to consult about the latest trend.

References

- Arbetter, Lisa (2003). <u>In Style: Secrets of Style, the complete guide to dressing your best every day.</u> New York, NY. Melcher M.

- Campbell, D. (1974). <u>If You Don't Know Where You're Going, You'll Probably End Up Somewhere Else.</u> Niles, ILL: Argus Communications

- Dove (2004). "The Real Truth About Beauty: A Global Report. Dr Nancy Etcoff and Dr Susie Orbach

- Feldon, Leah (2000). <u>Does This Make Me Look Fat? The definitive rules for dressing thin.</u> Villard, New York: Villard Books, registered trademark by Random House, Inc.

- Gawain, S. (1979). <u>Creative Visualization.</u> Berkeley, CA: Whatever Publishing

- Laney, Darlene (2008). And He Made a Woman, How to Become a Woman of Quality in a "B" Class World. Mobile, AL: Axiom Press

- McGrane, W.J. (1996). <u>Brighten Your Day With Self-Esteem.</u> Hummelstown, PA: Success Publishers, Markowshi International Publishers

- Monroe, Miles (1992). <u>Releasing Your Potential</u>. Shippensburg, PA. Destiny Image Publishers

- Stong's Concordance (1984). Nashville, TN. Thomas Nelson Publishers

- Successories of Illinois. (1993) <u>Follow Your Dreams.</u> Lombard, Illinois

- Webster's New World Dictionary of the American Language, 2nd College Edition, (1980) Simon & Shuster, New York, N.Y.

- Ziggler, Zig (1989). <u>See You At the Top.</u> Gretna, LA. Pelican Publishing Company, Inc.

Web Sources:
- Teen Help.com. (2012). Teen Development of Morals & Values. Source: nichd.nih.gov/new/ releases/religious.

- Teens and Plastic Surgery. May 2012. www.WebMD.SOURCES: American Society of Plastic Surgeons web site: "Plastic Surgery for Teenagers." Enhancement Media.com web site: "Plastic Surgery for Teens." MedicineNet web site: "Is Plastic Surgery a Teen Thing?"
- Body Care/Skin Care
  http://www.bodymatters.com

Etiquette
- http://www.etiquett-school.com
- Here's Information You Can Use,
  http://www.didyouknow.cd/info/tablesettings/htlm)
- http://www.chictechniques

Face Facts
- http://www.stylemakeover.com

Food Pyramid
- http://www.kidshealth.org
- http://www.lifeclinic.com/focus/nutrition/food-pyramid
- Article by: Tracey Allison Planinz, December 20, 2009
  http://www.livestrong.com/article/63067-pyramid-teens/#ixzz2AA7JpKJN
- A Word About Portion Control. www.pandaloveschristmas

Goal Setting:
- http://www.sie.edu/SPIN/activity.html
- http://iss.stthomas.edu/study/guides

Request for "Certificate of Completion"

Please complete the form as indicated. Be sure to print legibly as name will appear on certificate exactly as indicated.

I _____ verify and attest that _____

_____ has completed the GSF Program.

(Please print)

_____   _____

Name (signature required)   Date

Send to: God's Special Forces – P.O. Box 3654, Pinedale, California 93750-3654

----

www.ingramcontent.com/pod-product-compliance
Lightning Source LLC
Chambersburg PA
CBHW050658110426
42739CB00035B/3452